STUART ULLMAN

MW00845741

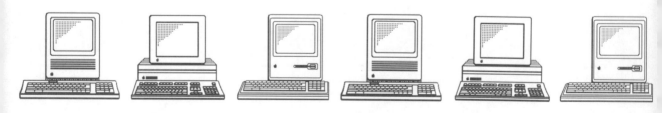

Macintosh® Programmer's Introduction to the Macintosh Family

Addison-Wesley Publishing Company, Inc.

Reading, Massachusetts   Menlo Park, California   New York
Don Mills, Ontario   Wokingham, England   Amsterdam   Bonn   Sydney
Singapore   Tokyo   Madrid   San Juan

Contents

Chapter 3   **An Eventful Experience 29**

Chapter 4   **Memory Management 41**

Chapter 5   **Display and Graphics Routines 59**

Chapter 7   **File Management 121**

Chapter 8   **Development Tools 135**

Figures and tables

Preface

Welcome to *Programmer's Introduction to the Macintosh Family*

Programmer's Introduction to the Macintosh Family is written for the experienced professional programmer who plans to design and develop applications for any members of the Apple® Macintosh® family of computers or is evaluating such a decision. Its purpose is to provide you with a conceptual framework for understanding the technical operation of the Macintosh family. Rather than being a programming manual, it is a programmer's technical overview of the powerful and flexible features encompassed by the Macintosh.

This book introduces the most important ideas, the most frequently used User Interface Toolbox calls, and the main programming features of the Macintosh. It performs a first-level screening of the more than 900 built-in Toolbox and Operating System routines and delineates those you should know well. It takes the same approach to the dozens of managers and packages that make up the Macintosh system software, focusing your attention on those with which you should begin your Macintosh programming experience.

Programmers whose background includes MS-DOS, AT&T UNIX®, or Apple II program development will find this book especially useful as it draws parallels between those experiences and Macintosh programming.

It is not necessary that you have any Macintosh programming experience to use this book. It makes only two assumptions about you as a reader:

□ You are assumed to be an experienced programmer to whom explanations of basic ideas like loops, procedures, calls, parameters, and results are not required.

□ You are assumed to have seen a Macintosh application in use. It would be helpful if you had used a Macintosh, not necessarily as a programmer but as a user familiar with the look and feel of the machine.

If you find yourself bewildered by concepts foreign to your experience, you should probably stop reading this manual and begin your study of the Macintosh with *Technical Introduction to the Macintosh Family,* also from Apple Computer.

What this book contains

This book has nine chapters and three appendixes. They are described briefly in the following paragraphs.

Chapter 1, "An Overview of the Macintosh," introduces the Macintosh family, addresses the question *Why program for the Macintosh?* and presents the key programming ideas that make the Macintosh a more powerful tool for programmers and users than earlier microcomputers.

Chapter 2, "The Software Anatomy of the Macintosh," is an overview of software architecture. It introduces resources, the User Interface Toolbox, and the Macintosh Operating System. It also offers some thoughts about program design and how it differs in the Macintosh environment.

Chapter 3, "An Eventful Experience," presents the concept of the main event loop, a central idea in Macintosh programming. It describes the loop, what must be in it, and how its requirements relate to your application programs.

Chapter 4, "Memory Management," is a conceptual and practical look at one of the most important and often troublesome aspects of the Macintosh. Here, you'll learn how and when objects stored in memory are subject to being relocated, how you can know precisely when they might be moved, and how to keep track of them.

Chapter 5, "Display and Graphics Routines," covers QuickDraw and Color QuickDraw routines.

Chapter 6, "The User Interface Toolbox," describes the four key managers and one important set of tools with which every Macintosh programmer must become familiar: the Window Manager, the Menu Manager, the Dialog Manager, the Control Manager, and TextEdit.

Chapter 7, "File Management," explains how files are organized, how the user accesses them, and how your program creates, opens, reads, writes, and closes disk files.

Chapter 8, "Development Tools," offers an overview of the Macintosh Programmer's Workshop (MPW) and MacApp™, two Apple Computer development environments for the Macintosh.

Chapter 9, "Becoming a Macintosh Developer," prepares you for the next steps in your education as a Macintosh programmer. It tells you about the organization of the "bible" of Macintosh programming, *Inside Macintosh*. It also addresses issues like registering as a developer and obtaining technical support.

Appendix A, "Compatibility Issues and Guidelines," discusses important issues of compatibility across Macintosh family members. Guidelines for ensuring compatibility with future systems are also provided.

Appendix B, "Important Operating System and Toolbox Calls," presents the most frequently needed calls in an easy-to-find format.

Appendix C, "The Apple Programmer's and Developer's Association," tells you about APDA: why it exists, how it operates, what its relation is to Apple Computer, and the services it provides to developers.

About Macintosh technical documentation

Apple Computer has produced several books that explain the hardware and software of the Macintosh family of computers. There are *Inside Macintosh* Volumes I through V, books about single aspects of the Macintosh, introductory books, and Macintosh-related books.

The original Macintosh documentation consisted solely of the noble tome *Inside Macintosh,* a three-volume compendium covering the whole of the Macintosh Toolbox and Operating System for the original 64K Macintosh ROM, together with user interface guidelines and hardware information. With the introduction of the Macintosh Plus (128K ROM), Volume IV of *Inside Macintosh* was released. A fifth volume has now been added, covering the Macintosh SE and Macintosh II computers (both containing 256K of ROM). Volumes IV and V are delta guides; that is, they explain only what is different about the new machines. Taken all together, the five volumes of *Inside Macintosh* provide a comprehensive reference for the Macintosh family computers.

With the growth of the Macintosh family, some of the material in *Inside Macintosh* is starting to appear in single-subject books. Each of those books provides complete information about its subject, including information that may appear in one or more volumes of *Inside Macintosh*.

For people who are new to the Macintosh world, Apple has created two introductory books: *Technical Introduction to the Macintosh Family* and this book, *Programmer's Introduction to the Macintosh Family*. These books provide explanation and guidelines for using the features described in *Inside Macintosh*.

In addition to the books about the Macintosh itself, there are books on related subjects, including books about the user interface and Apple's floating-point numerics, and the reference books for the Macintosh Programmer's Workshop.

Figure P-1 illustrates the road map of the Macintosh technical documentation. The paths in the road map show the relationships among the books. Table P-1 gives a brief description of each book in the set.

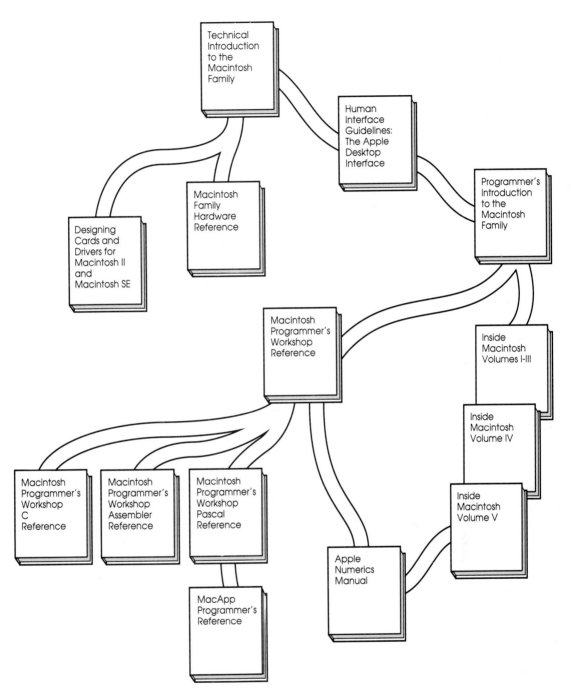

Figure P-1
A road map to Macintosh technical documentation

Table P-1
A summary of Macintosh technical documentation

Original *Inside Macintosh:*

Inside Macintosh, Volumes I–III — Complete reference to the Macintosh Toolbox and Operating System for the original 64K ROM.

Inside Macintosh, Volumes IV — Delta guide to the Macintosh Plus (128K ROM).

Inside Macintosh, Volumes V — Delta guide to the Macintosh SE and Macintosh II (256K ROM versions).

Introductory books:

Technical Introduction to the Macintosh Family — Introduction to the Macintosh software and hardware for all Macintosh computers: the original Macintosh, Macintosh Plus, Macintosh SE, and Macintosh II.

Programmer's Introduction to the Macintosh Family — Introduction to programming the Macintosh system for programmers who are new to it.

Single-subject books:

Macintosh Family Hardware Reference — Reference to the Macintosh hardware for all Macintosh computers, excluding the Macintosh XL.

Designing Cards and Drivers for the Macintosh II and Macintosh SE — Hardware and device driver reference to the expansion capabilities of the Macintosh II and the Macintosh SE.

Related books:

Human Interface Guidelines: The Apple Desktop Interface — Detailed guidelines for developers implementing the Macintosh user interface.

Apple Numerics Manual — Description of the Standard Apple Numerics Environment (SANE), an IEEE-standard floating-point environment supported by all Apple computers.

Macintosh Programmer's Workshop 2.0 Reference — Description of the Macintosh Programmer's Workshop (MPW), Apple's software development environment for all Macintosh computers.

Some conventions

This book discusses several generations of Macintosh computers, describing their similarities and differences. The following terminological conventions have been adopted to clarify the discussion:

- Unless otherwise indicated, the discussion refers to all Macintosh computers. The term *Macintosh* is used generically to refer to the entire product line.

- Unless otherwise indicated, information relating to the Macintosh Plus also holds true for the original 128K Macintosh, the Macintosh 512K, and the 512K enhanced. These are sometimes called collectively the *classic Macintosh*.

- ❖ *Note:* The Macintosh XL differs in many respects from the other members of the Macintosh family and is not described in this book. The Macintosh XL is based on the Lisa hardware, with RAM-based software that emulates the operation of the Macintosh 64K ROM.

Numerous special terms are introduced throughout this book. Terms appearing in **boldface** are defined in the glossary at the end of the book.

In the text, the names of Operating System and Toolbox calls appear in `Courier` typeface.

Most of the computer program examples in this book are written in a pseudo-code rather than in any conventional computer programming language. In such listings, the names of Operating System and Toolbox calls and predefined constants appear in **boldface** so that you can determine which calls are part of the Macintosh and which you are assumed to have supplied elsewhere.

Chapter 1

An Overview of the Macintosh

This chapter briefly introduces key ideas that recur throughout the book. It also provides a framework for understanding the various models of Macintosh for which you might want to develop programs.

Why program for the Macintosh family?

The fact that you are reading this book means that you have probably already decided to develop software for the Macintosh family. At least, it indicates that you are considering doing so. For the record, though, let's present some of the main reasons you, an experienced programmer, might want to jump on board the Macintosh bandwagon. There are dozens of reasons, but we'll focus on just four main ones: development power, pride in applications, a growing installed base, and the value of working on the leading edge.

Powerful system and development tools

Every major computer language has been implemented on the Macintosh, along with quite a few not so major ones. In addition, its natural windowing environment offers a powerful and easy-to-use way of developing programs. You can watch execution in one window while you examine code in another and track output in yet another.

With the Macintosh Programmer's Workshop (MPW) and MacApp (an object-oriented template program from which to begin your development), Apple offers powerful development tools on the Macintosh backed by Apple's highly regarded technical support for developers. Both of these tools are discussed in Chapter 8.

But the power of the Macintosh doesn't stop when application development is complete. The user also sees the Macintosh as a powerful machine. With a high-speed microprocessor at its heart and 1 megabyte of memory standard, with hard disks capable of storing dozens of megabytes of data, and with powerful software, the Macintosh is a serious business machine.

Pride in applications

There are thousands of programs that run on the Macintosh. They range from spreadsheets to games, from powerful relational data bases to telecommunications programs, from drafting and drawing programs to desktop publishing tools. But good Macintosh applications have at least two things in common:

□ They are consistently easy to use because of their highly standardized and usable interface.

□ They *look* great.

When you show off your Macintosh software to fellow programmers, potential investors, prospective buyers, and others, you will be able to take pride in the way your programs look. They have a finished, polished, no-nonsense air about them, yet they look easy and fun to use.

A fast-growing installed base

The Macintosh has the fastest-growing installed base of any personal computer system on the market. In early 1987, it became the leading seller among personal computer systems. There are millions of Macintosh systems installed, and the rate of installation continues to climb.

Installed base translates into potential buyers, which in turn translates into potential profits for the software entrepreneur or publisher who recognizes the trend.

The leading edge

One operating system supports all models of the Macintosh, and Apple is committed to ensuring that future machines remain equally compatible at the operating-system level.

Macintosh systems already offer concurrency of operation under MultiFinder, with foreground and background tasking that remain distant possibilities for other microcomputer systems.

When you work with the Macintosh, you will not experience media incompatibility headaches, either. All Macintoshes run with the 3.5-inch disk that has become the industry standard. A disk created on a Macintosh Plus can be read on a Macintosh II with no modifications or gymnastics.

There are no artificial limitations on memory and disk capacity with the Macintosh family. The entire addressability range of the powerful processors is available to the system.

Finally, the bus architecture of the Macintosh II is an advanced, easy-to-use feature. The NuBus is the bus of the future.

The Macintosh has already embodied a powerful operating system with a full-blown development environment. It is the leading-edge microcomputer.

A look at the Macintosh family

Table 1-1 summarizes the key features of the Macintosh 512K, Macintosh Plus, Macintosh SE, and Macintosh II computers.

Table 1-1
Comparing the main members of the Macintosh family

Characteristic	Macintosh 512K	Macintosh Plus	Macintosh SE	Macintosh II
Processor	68000	68000	68000	68020
RAM (standard)	512K	1 MB	1 MB	1 MB
RAM (expanded)	512K	4 MB	4 MB	8 MB
Address bus	24-bit	24-bit	24-bit	24/32-bit
Clock speed	7.8 MHz	7.8 MHz	7.8 MHz	15.7 MHz
ROM	128K	128K	256K	256K
3.5-inch disk	Internal, 800K	Internal, 800K	1 or 2 internal, 800K	1 or 2 internal, 800K
Video	9-inch, mono	9-inch, mono	9-inch, mono	Separate monitor/ video card
Keyboard and mouse	Direct connect	Direct connect	ADB	ADB

Types of programs

There are at least four basic types of programs you might consider developing for the Macintosh. Three of them have direct parallels in other microcomputer environments. These are end-user applications, device drivers, and development tools. As you would expect, device drivers and programming languages and tools are among the most complex types of programs to develop for the Macintosh (or for any other computer, for that matter). It is most likely that your work will be on end-user applications such as accounting programs, word processors, spreadsheets, communications programs, and data bases.

The fourth type of application is the **desk accessory.** If you've used a Macintosh, you have almost certainly used at least one desk accessory. These are stand-alone programs, usually small but not necessarily so, that the user can call upon any time, even in the middle of running another application. The user simply points at the Apple icon in the upper left corner of the screen, opens it, and selects the desk accessory to use. It then becomes the current application until the user closes it or activates another desk accessory or application.

Many beginning Macintosh programmers are tempted to design a desk accessory as their first project. Their generally small size and focused purposes can be deceiving, though. Writing a desk accessory is not easier than writing any other kind of end-user application. In some ways, it is more difficult.

The key programming ideas

Most of this book is about how to program the Macintosh family. It presents basic techniques, explains main programming features, and outlines design approaches. This discussion takes place against the backdrop of some central ideas in Macintosh programming. These can be stated as aphorisms:

☐ The user is the boss.

☐ Compatibility is the path of least resistance.

☐ Nobody does it from scratch.

The user plays a central role

The Macintosh is designed to make the user the boss. Everything that happens in the system happens because the user asks for it to, directly or indirectly. This is the single most important concept in Macintosh programming. And it has wide-ranging ramifications.

Two other central programming ideas emerge from this basic philosophy: the user interface design and event-driven programming.

User interface design

Apple believes so strongly that the user is central that it has published a book called *Human Interface Guidelines: The Apple Desktop Interface.* If you don't yet have a copy, get one soon. It may be a good idea not to start programming your first application until reading and digesting it if you are writing your program for other people to use.

Suggestions on how to use menus, when and how to change windows, where to put dialog and alert boxes and what they should say, are contained in the guidelines. Users expect the programs they buy for their Macintosh systems to follow these guidelines.

This idea—that the computer manufacturer should set forth the principles by which programs interface with the user—is new and some programmers have stumbled over it. But two facts are undeniable:

☐ The vast majority of Macintosh applications follow the guidelines closely (though probably none does completely).

☐ Programs that deviate seriously from the guidelines, without a good reason the user can understand, don't sell as well and cause more support headaches for their publishers than those that follow the rules.

In other microcomputers, a "well-behaved" program is one that doesn't conflict with other programs' use of memory or the display screen. In Macintosh, it is one that a first-time user can pick up and begin to understand without spending dozens of hours.

Event-driven programming

Of all the conceptual models of programming, the one that best describes how a Macintosh program looks and works is that of the Grand Funnel (see Figure 1-1).

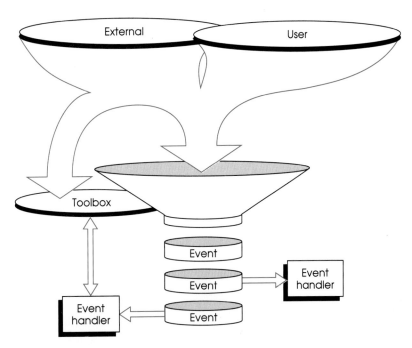

Figure 1-1
The Grand Funnel

At the top of the funnel is the user, running your program. The user produces events by interacting with the system and with your program. In addition, external activities such as network interactions and disks being inserted also produce events. As these events pass through the funnel, they are prioritized automatically by the Event Manager. (In the world of Macintosh system software, "manager" refers to groups of routines that provide a particular type of functionality.) Your program examines each event, determines what type it is, and passes it to the appropriate event handler. Some of these event handlers, in turn, produce their own events, which go back into the top of the funnel. This ebb and flow of control and interaction resembles a real-time programming environment in which your program must field and deal with a wide range of events, often happening with great rapidity.

The user is the primary—practically the sole—generator of events. Your program spends much of its time in its main event loop, waiting for a new event to manage.

This becomes much clearer in Chapter 3, where the main event loop is explained.

Compatibility is easy; incompatibility is not

With most computer systems, compatibility is a constant worry for the programmer as well as the user. If you put an item into memory at an unused location today, will that location still be unused in two years when the new model comes out? What if the keyboard on the new system is radically different? Will the pro-gram have to change to accommodate it? The issue plagues you.

With the Macintosh, being compatible is easy. Designing a program so that it is *not* compatible takes extra effort. All of the Macintosh Toolbox ROMs have been upward compatible. Routines written to run on a 128K machine (the no-longer-manufactured original Macintosh) run on the 512K Macintosh, the Macintosh Plus, the Macintosh SE, and the Macintosh II *without any changes.*

If your programs follow Apple's guidelines, they will run on future versions of Macintosh family hardware. Only by doing something totally nonstandard would you make your program unusable on any new member of the family. Appendix A discusses the important guidelines you should follow to ensure compatibility.

Templates ease programming

An interesting thing happened early in Macintosh programming circles. Programmers began to realize that the main event loop was a highly reusable piece of code if it was handled right. Pretty quickly, most Macintosh programmers were using main event loops written by other Macintosh programmers and modifying them to suit their applications' needs.

Not only is that still true, but Apple has made it even easier than before to do this kind of borrowing. Apple has published MacApp, a generic application written in a powerful version of Pascal. Macintosh developers are using this environment to accelerate program development and to ensure further the consistency of program user interfaces.

Chapter 2

The Software Anatomy of the Macintosh

This chapter discusses the software architecture of the Macintosh. It begins with a presentation of the fundamental ways the Macintosh differs from other microcomputers. It then points out the main components of the system's architecture and how these pieces fit together, and focuses on each component from the programmer's perspective.

The chapter closes with a discussion of some programming tasks that you would customarily perform at the end of your assignment but should be considered earlier when developing a Macintosh application.

An architectural overview

Modern application programmers try to make a microcomputer system's components transparent to the user. To do so, programmers must manage displays, printers, memory, disk-based file systems, and user input devices as unobtrusively to the user as possible. This management requires a wide variety of tools and languages.

But this desire to design "user-transparent" solutions conflicts with the modern programming trend toward higher levels of abstraction. Symbolic and object-oriented programming are becoming more significant in programming. Your dilemma, then, is that you must manage infinitesimal details of memory and disk file access while attempting to maintain a broad overview of the user's needs and desires.

The Macintosh is an evolutionary step in the direction of providing you with the kinds of tools that make designing user-transparent solutions as "programmer-friendly" as possible.

At the same time, the Macintosh permits you to give the user greater control over the system. In fact, it requires such trust by its very design. By passing on to the user the responsibility for certain tasks, the Macintosh permits the programmer to focus on the more conceptual aspects of solving the user's problem.

Figure 2-1 illustrates some of the differences between the Macintosh and other microcomputers from the perspective of the programmer. The first part of the figure depicts the model most programmers have learned. Using this approach, the programmer must be concerned with skillfully blending all relevant elements of the system into a finished application that isolates the user from the system as much as possible. In the second part of the figure, the Macintosh model shows that the programmer has a number of powerful tools in the User Interface Toolbox and in resources that combine to create user applications. In addition, the programmer interacts with the Macintosh Operating System and with something called the **Finder**™. The user, meanwhile, interacts with the application program and also with the Finder. The Toolbox and resources together make up the techniques for handling all of the components enclosed in the dotted line in the first model.

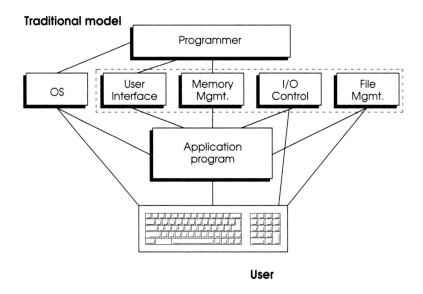

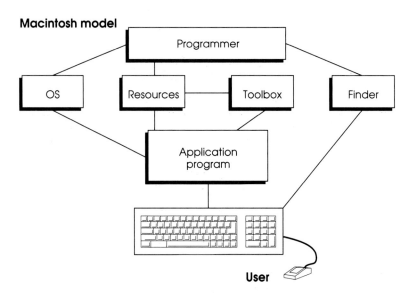

Figure 2-1
Two programming models

The Macintosh model makes programming easier while making the resulting applications easier to use. This is all in keeping with the basic principles discussed in Chapter 1.

" *The Toolbox itself is a very good model of how to program the Macintosh. It's made up of small, largely stand-alone functions.* "

Gerhard Schulten,
Apple Computer
author of MacDraw 2.0

The pieces

You will find yourself spending the bulk of your Macintosh programming time working with the User Interface Toolbox. Occasionally, you will use the Toolbox (as it is also known) to create and manage resources. Viewed simplistically, a Macintosh program consists of a collection of Toolbox calls, some of which manipulate **resources.** These elements are then combined with your application's specific data processing procedures. As with all computer programs, this processing is largely transparent to the user.

Compared with most programming you have done, you will find yourself involved relatively infrequently with the Operating System and with memory and disk file management. Even when you do interact with those parts of the Macintosh system, you will do so at a higher level than you are accumstomed to. Battling with bits and bytes, complex memory segmentation and addressing schemes, and device-dependent I/O becomes a thing of the past.

Putting the pieces together

Figure 2-2 shows the relationships among the main pieces of the Macintosh system software architecture. There is a high degree of interdependence among the components. QuickDraw plays a central role, as you will see in Chapter 5. There is also a definite hierarchy within some of the components.

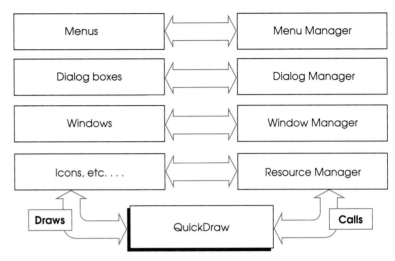

Figure 2-2
Macintosh system software architecture

This will make more sense by the time you finish reading this chapter. For the moment, it is only important that you understand that the components of the Macintosh software architecture are primarily tools and managers assigned to manage specific aspects of the user interface. They relate to one another in two ways:

☐ The manager uses QuickDraw, the basic Macintosh drawing utilities, to display each interface element.

☐ An activity involving any of these elements is handled by calls to the responsible manager.

The other portions of the Macintosh software architecture play more traditional roles. The Memory Manager operates in a different way from most memory control systems, but its fundamental task is nonetheless to manage memory. Similarly, the File Manager enables your program to deal with disk-based files. These managers are explained in more detail in Chapters 4 and 7, respectively.

The Toolbox

One of the most significant aspects of the Macintosh's software anatomy programmer is the User Interface Toolbox, or Toolbox for short. This section contains a brief overview of the Toolbox utilities; a more in-depth discussion of the significant calls and their usage appears in Chapter 6.

What is the Toolbox?

Conceptually, you can think of the Toolbox as a **library** of procedures and functions that your program can use without having to spend a lot of time re-inventing the wheel. On conventional microcomputers, it is fairly common to spend hundreds or even thousands of dollars acquiring libraries of routines written in the language with which you are working. C and Pascal libraries abound. They range from very specific libraries which carry out narrow sets of tasks such as graphic displays or complex mathematics to broad-based libraries designed to provide a kind of "cookbook" of functions.

With the Macintosh, you don't need to go out and find, evaluate, purchase, load, and implement such libraries. Apple has supplied a powerful library for you.

What's in the Toolbox?

Figure 2-3 shows the parts of the Toolbox and their approximate hierarchical relation to one another. The components nearer the top of the figure quite often call those below them in the hierarchy. The relationship is not rigid, however, and it is possible for lower level routines sometimes to call or use higher level ones.

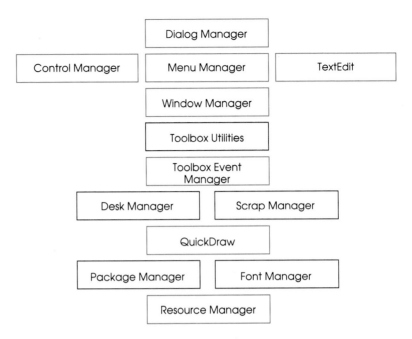

Figure 2-3
The hierarchical order of Toolbox parts

The shaded routines in Figure 2-3 are discussed in greater detail in Chapter 6. QuickDraw and Color QuickDraw routines are the subject of Chapter 5. You will need the others less frequently. When you do need information about them, refer to *Inside Macintosh*.

For a discussion of the basic functions of each of the elements in the Toolbox, see *Technical Introduction to the Macintosh Family*.

Why use Toolbox routines?

Toolbox routines such as those described here and in Chapters 5 and 6 enable you to provide the consistency of interface that is such an important part of the Macintosh world. Furthermore, using these calls guarantees that your programs will continue to operate as expected on future versions of Macintosh. In other words, you don't need to worry excessively about compatibility.

Beyond those basic reasons, there is at least one other good reason to use the Toolbox routines rather than designing your own to handle such things as menus, windows, and dialog boxes even though it is perfectly possible to do so if you wish. Quite simply, it is easier to *use* them than to circumvent them. Working around the Toolbox routines to write your own code takes more code and more energy and introduces more bugs. Because the Toolbox routines are largely in ROM and are highly optimized, you won't find yourself gaining any real execution speed. And the potential incompatibility problems you create for yourself are just not worth the effort.

Marshalling your resources

One of the most powerful and innovative ideas in the Macintosh programmer's world is the **resource.** Simply stated, nearly everything that is stored in a Macintosh is or can be a resource. Resources provide Macintosh programmers with great flexibility, make their programs adaptable to foreign-language implementation, and generally make life easier.

What is a resource?

In his book *How to Write Macintosh Software* (Hayden, 1986), Scott Knaster says: "If you ask a Macintosh programmer what a resource is, you're likely to be told, 'Everything is a resource!'" As he points out, "That's close."

Simply put, your program sees a resource as any bits and pieces it needs to do its job. For the most part, resources are displayed to the user. Menus, dialog boxes, and controls are all resources. Their original purpose was to facilitate the transfer of Macintosh programs between speakers of different languages. Because a resource is not "hard coded" into your program, translating it into another language can be undertaken by a nonprogrammer.

The list of options (words and phrases) that make up a menu constitutes a single resource. So, too, does a set of numbers that define the dimensions of a window. Scroll bars, icons, dialog boxes and their contents, the cursors used by an application, and dozens of other small pieces of data and program code are resources. In fact, your program's code is even a resource.

Resources and your program

Resources are stored in application program files on the disk (see Chapter 7). The Macintosh uses an index called the **resource map,** which is very much like a header record in a more conventional disk file. This map contains information that permits the Macintosh to view the stream of bits stored in a portion of the file as individual resources with beginning and ending points in the stream. The job of interpreting this map and picking out the resources to which it points falls to the Resource Manager.

There are a number of means for creating resources. In some cases, you can design a resource interactively in much the way you draw or paint objects using MacPaint™. In others, you write text descriptions of the resources and let the Resource Manager figure out how to display them when your program runs. Much of the decision is a function of the development system or environment you are using. More information on creating resources can be found in Chapter 6 in the discussions of each type of resource and its use.

Using calls to the Resource Manager, your program brings in dialog boxes, menus, icons, and other, similar objects. Your program need not be concerned with whether a resource it needs is already in memory or stored on disk because the Resource Manager handles management for the program.

Memory Manager
Segment Loader
OS Event Manager
File Manager
Device Manager
Disk Driver
Sound Driver
ROM Serial Driver
Vertical Retrace Driver
System Error Handler
OS Utilities

Figure 2-4
The components of the
Macintosh Operating System

The Macintosh Operating System

Contrary to what you may have heard, the Macintosh really does have an operating system. *Inside Macintosh* says it well: "As the Toolbox is your program's interface to the user, the Operating System is its interface to the Macintosh." Don't confuse the Operating System in the Macintosh's ROMs with the System icon on your desktop. The System file is more appropriately thought of as the system *resource* file. It contains resources shared by all applications. Figure 2-4 shows the components of the Operating System. Unlike the User Interface Toolbox routines, there is no particular hierarchical order to these components. The parts of the Operating System highlighted in Figure 2-4 are discussed later in this book.

The Macintosh Operating System does not differ radically in function from other operating systems with which you may be familiar. Low-level, hardware-related events like mouse-button presses and keystrokes are handled here, as are file and serial device I/O, sound, network and other interface drivers, and a number of other functions.

When programming the Macintosh, one of the most important parts of the Operating System is the Memory Manager, discussed in Chapter 4.

But the way you use the Macintosh Operating System differs markedly from the way you are accustomed to making other microcomputer operating-system calls. In other systems, most operating-system interface takes place by means of direct-memory addressing using either subroutine jumps or interrupts. This direct-memory approach has a perceived advantage of speed but is hobbled as a design strategy because the next generation of the operating system may change some interrupt vectors or other vital information. The result is a neccssity to debug and revise code each time the operating system changes.

On the Macintosh, you interact with the Operating System by means of utility calls and other calls that closely resemble the User Interface Toolbox routines. In fact, there are many operational similarities between the Operating System and the User Interface Toolbox.

The Finder

Most Macintosh system disks contain at least two items: a System file (discussed in the preceding section) and a Finder. The Finder, however, is not required to boot a disk on the Macintosh. On most system disks, if the Finder is present it is the *startup application,* meaning that it is the first application called when the system is started up using that disk. The Finder is responsible for presenting the familiar desktop that greets most Macintosh users when they start their machines.

The Finder and the user

The Finder is in many ways an application. It is only slightly different from the ordinary Macintosh application in that its role is file and desktop management. With the Finder, the user can set up folders, move files around, rename them, copy them, or delete them. These are functions you are accustomed to thinking of as being handled through an operating system. They are also functions you frequently programmed into your applications in the past because the user might well need to manage files as a part of using your program.

On the Macintosh, the user is given control over and responsibility for file management. The Finder is a tool for handling the tasks. Most well-designed Macintosh applications do not include the ability to delete, rename, copy, or otherwise manipulate files while they are running.

The Finder is also the place from which the user chooses an application and starts it. When the user finishes running your application and chooses to quit, the system returns to the Finder (assuming Finder is the startup application).

The Finder and your application

While your application is running, it typically has nothing to do with the Finder. In fact, the Finder is almost certainly not in memory when your program is running unless the user is running your program under MultiFinder or a similar application.

During development, however, your program must be aware of the Finder. Because the user interacts with your program first at the Finder level, your program must make itself known to the Finder as an application available to run. It must also identify documents associated with it so that if the user double-clicks on a document icon belonging to your program, the Finder understands that the user wants to start your program and open that document.

Thinking about "last" things first

One crucial difference between programming the Macintosh and programming more traditional microcomputers is the order in which you should take into account various kinds of operations. Specifically, there are several functions that would be usual practice to leave to the last phase of development. These include printing operations, the Undo routine, the user interface design, and localization of the user interface.

On the Macintosh, if you leave these kinds of functions to the end of the programming cycle, you may find what you would have thought would be very easy tasks occupying a significant amount of time and energy.

This section discusses these aspects of Macintosh programming with an eye not toward teaching you how to carry them out in great detail but rather toward helping you focus on the important design issues they raise early in the software development cycle.

Printing functions and the Printing Manager

In the traditional microcomputer programming world, printing is a simple task. It is also boring and somewhat limited. Macintosh takes out the boring limitations. In the process, it requires you to take a closer look at the printing process and to give more thought to it at the beginning of program development.

Macintosh printing has two features that are normally not part of microcomputer programs:

☐ printer independence

☐ bit-mapped graphics output for all types of documents

Printer independence

The Printing Manager makes it possible for your program to largely ignore the type of printer being used. It stores the codes that drive the printer in a separate printer resource file on the user's disk. Included within that file is a printer driver used by the Operating System to communicate between the Printing Manager and the printer.

This printer independence is a boon to the programmer. No longer will you have to design and write dozens—even hundreds—of separate files to accommodate various printers in your application. Users can buy collections of printer drivers that permit them to use the printers they own in any application they want. Your application need not change, regardless of which printer the user selects.

But every silver lining has a cloud. The down side of this is that you must not make rash assumptions about the capabilities of the printer on the other end of the application. Or, if your application must make such assumptions, you must notify the user, preferably both in the documentation and in the program itself at the start of a printing operation.

Bit-mapped graphics everywhere

Most printers used with the Macintosh are either dot matrix printers or laser printers. Both of these use bit-mapped graphics almost exclusively for output. Because of that, and because of the way the Printing Manager looks at the world, a Macintosh uses QuickDraw graphics routines (see Chapter 5) to prepare the document for printing.

In essence, printing a page on a dot matrix or laser printer involves many of the same processes as drawing that same page on the display.

The Undo routine

Before the Macintosh, most microcomputer applications did not include the ability for users to change their minds about something after they'd done it. Even popular word processors lacked this capability. Part of the reason is that keeping careful track of what the user is doing is not an easy task. And without it, undoing what has been done becomes impossible.

Unlike almost everything else you program on the Macintosh, there is no built-in routine to call for undoing something. You have to roll your own undo routine.

But Macintosh users are accustomed to being able to undo actions, particularly editing steps. In fact, there is a general agreement among users that if an action alters the contents of a document, it should be immediately undoable. Any other operation—such as choosing a menu command, loading a file, or closing a window—is generally not undoable.

Because Undo is a roll-your-own application routine and calls for careful planning, you must decide at the beginning of your design cycle what, if any, functions will be undoable. Then you must program your application so that it keeps track of what the user is doing, stores information in a buffer so that it can easily be recalled to undo the effects of an operation, and generally manages things cleanly with respect to the Undo operation.

User interface design

It is surprising how many programmers forget to focus on the user interface design until all their routines are working and debugged. Then, as part of the final program assembly, they try to "glue" it together with interface design.

That approach on the Macintosh is a virtual guarantee of frustration and possible failure.

The user interface is the most important aspect in the design of a Macintosh program, and it is essential that you understand how you expect users to interact with the program before you try to write the code.

In traditional microcomputer programming, not only could the user interface be left to last in the development cycle, but it was probably *better* to do so. For example, if a series of nested menus—a classic "user-friendly" interface, pre-Macintosh—was designed first and then the program evolved, the menus often needed changing. And menu changes virtually always required programming changes. It was much better to let the program's functional parts solidify and then write the user interface around what was actually being implemented.

On the Macintosh, the opposite is true. In the first place, because the programs are driven by user events, the user interface is the most important part of the program, not an afterthought to make the program marketable. Second, changing the user interface is fairly simple and straightforward, requiring minimal programming changes. In fact, if the programmer uses appropriate tools, the user interface is so easy to change that even the user can modify it after the product is delivered and in use.

Localization

Between resources and the Toolbox, a Macintosh programmer has all the necessary components to make programs easy to move into other languages and cultures. The process of "localization" of your programs will be easy to accomplish and will pay great dividends if you follow a few simple rules. (For more information, see *Human Interface Guidelines,* which contains an appendix on the subject of localization.)

The general principle is to use Apple system resources where they are available. For example, in date-time formatting, sort sequences, and numeric punctuation, Apple's international resources are set up so that they are correct in the country in which the computer was sold. If you use those resources instead of coding such items directly in your program, users in the United States will see a numeric value as 23,789.04, and European users will see it as 23.789,04.

Another sound principle is to avoid having your program rely on strings being a specific length. After these strings (which you should have stored as resources) are translated, they will almost never be the same length.

Using low-memory global variables rather than hard coding to determine such things as menu bar height will also make your programs easier to write and maintain. In some countries, the size of the menu bar and the system font and size are different from what they are on U.S. machines. This is due to the need for higher resolution in non-Roman characters (such as Japanese kanji) and other international differences.

Finally, use the International Utilities Package and its sorting, currency, measurement, date, and time formatting routines. Where seemingly conflicting routines exist both in the User Interface Toolbox and in the International Utilities Package, use the latter. They tend to be more accurate, particularly as standards change.

There is much more to be said about localization, but the purpose of this discussion is simply to alert you to take the need for translation into account. If you store strings as resources, don't rely on them to be a predetermined length, and follow the other principles outlined here, you will be well on the road to writing Macintosh programs that can be used throughout the world.

Chapter 3

An Eventful Experience

No concept is more crucial to programming the Macintosh than the event loop. The Macintosh is an event-driven computer. It spends a great deal of its time in an all but endless loop, waiting for the user to do something that will trigger it into action. This chapter focuses on the event loop and on the Toolbox **Event Manager,** which manages the Macintosh's response to user-generated events.

An overview of the main event loop

Viewed from its outermost level, the main event loop in the Macintosh is a layered set of routines, as shown in Figure 3-1. It requires the execution of a series of initialization procedures before the loop is begun. The loop itself consists of a `GetNextEvent` call followed by a series of conditional clauses that identify the type of event involved and process it accordingly.

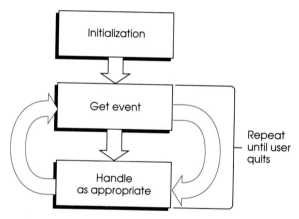

Figure 3-1
The outermost level of the main event loop

In Pascal, these conditional clauses are in the form of a series of Case statements. In C, the case-switch combination is the most often used mechanism for handling events.

Setting up the loop

Most Macintosh programs begin with two or three important initialization calls before the main event loop is entered. Before `InitWindows` can be called, you must have initialized the QuickDraw routines with a call to `InitGraf` and the Font Manager with the Toolbox call `InitFonts`. From the viewpoint of the Event Manager, the most important initialization routine is arguably `InitWindows`, which initializes the Window Manager. The data structures in the Window Manager are used by the Event Manager. If the Window Manager is not properly initialized, the Event Manager cannot do its job.

Another useful initialization call is `FlushEvents`. This call clears stray events left over from what took place before your application began running. For example, if the user double-clicks your application's icon and then presses one or more keys on the keyboard or clicks the mouse, these events are stored in the event queue (which is covered later in this chapter). Your program, however, should ignore these actions. `FlushEvents` with the proper arguments clears all events from the event queue and gives your program a clean area with which to begin its execution. This flushing of pending events is generally only done once, and only at the time your program initializes its environment.

The outer loop: How it works

The details of the loop's event handling are the subject of most of the rest of this chapter.

This outer loop waits for an event to occur. When one does occur, it handles the event in accordance with the type of event and the instructions associated with it in your program. When the event involves the user quitting the application, the loop ends, the application terminates, and the user is (typically) returned to the Finder. From there, the user can choose some other program to run or a document to edit.

When the `GetNextEvent` call is executed, the Event Manager issues an automatic call to the Desk Manager to determine if the event involved is a system event. If it is, the `GetNextEvent` routine returns a Boolean False value. Your program simply checks this Boolean value as part of the loop. If it finds it to be False, the event can be discarded because the system has already dealt with it.

The second level: What kind of event?

Within the portion of the outer loop labeled Handle, the next level of the main event loop determines the type of event.

The sequence in which these events appear in your program is not important. The Event Manager automatically returns the highest priority event when the `GetNextEvent` call is made.

By the use of event masks, discussed later in this chapter, you can block certain kinds of events from being acknowledged by your program. If a mask is in use, the Event Manager returns the highest priority event of those recognized by your program. This means that you can determine what kinds of events are important for your program to work with and how to deal with them. The Event Manager takes care of everything else automatically. (It is seldom if ever necessary to change the default event mask.)

Figure 3-2 lists the events in their order of priority.

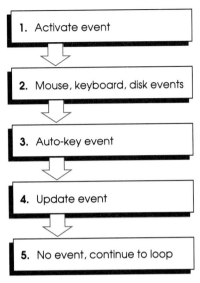

Figure 3-2
The event priority list

Activate events

An activate event occurs whenever a window is activated or deactivated. In any Macintosh application, only one window can be active at a time. A number of actions can change this active window. For example, the user might click the mouse in a window that is partially hidden behind the currently active window. Or your program might write text or draw graphics into a window that has not been the active window to that point.

Mouse events

The mouse is one of the main sources of events to which your main event loop has to respond. There are essentially two kinds of mouse events: mouse-down and mouse-up. You don't often have to deal with mouse-up events. To detect a double-click, your program need only determine if the mouse has been pressed twice within a preset time frame at the same place on the screen.

Key events

Aside from the mouse, most user-generated events originate at the keyboard. Most key events, of course, simply require that the character represented by the key be echoed to the screen in the currently active window using the current font information. But you must check to see if the Command key is also being pressed. If so, the user may be trying to execute a menu command without activating the menu bar. Such events are handled by the Menu Manager.

Similarly, the Caps Lock, Shift, and Option keys—collectively called *modifier keys*—can alter the intended effect of pressing a key. Your program must check for such combinations as part of its processing of key events in the main event loop.

If the user holds down a key or key combination for a few moments, you may have to respond to an auto-key event.

Disk-inserted events

If the user inserts a disk into a drive or mounts a new volume on a hard disk, a disk-inserted event is placed on the event queue. Typically, your program need not concern itself with this type of event because `GetNextEvent` takes care of most such occurrences. The Macintosh's built-in Standard File Package is designed to respond to them. If the disk inserted by the user is defective, unformatted (*uninitialized* in Macintosh parlance), or causes some other error, your program may have to call on the Disk Initialization Package's `DIBadMount` routine.

Update events

When it isn't responding to some other type of event, the Event Manager looks for windows whose contents require updating. This need can arise from user activities, program displays, or system-generated overlays of dialog boxes or other objects. These activities typically generate update events. Windows are checked front to back so that the active window is checked first and updated if necessary. Then the window behind the active window is checked, and so forth.

The third level: Mouse event handling

One level farther into the main event loop, your program approaches the basic handling of mouse-down events.

Locating the mouse

When the user presses the mouse button, the location of the mouse pointer is significant. For example, completely different processing of a mouse event is required if the pointer is in the menu bar rather than in an application's active window.

The first step in handling a mouse-down event is to find the location of the mouse pointer. This is accomplished with the FindWindow call. A call to this command will enable a Macintosh program to determine whether the mouse was pressed while the pointer was in

☐ a desk accessory window

☐ the menu bar

☐ an application window

A desk accessory window

If the mouse is pressed while the pointer is in a window belonging to a desk accessory, your application handles the event by calling the Desk Manager routine SystemClick. The system then passes control to the desk accessory that created and manages the window involved. When the processing is complete, control is returned to your application. This means that your program need know nothing about the desk accessories available to the user. It also means that your program will always be aware of the user's activation and deactivation of desk accessories.

The menu bar

If the mouse is pressed while in the menu bar, your application calls the Menu Manager's `MenuSelect` routine. This routine highlights the menu name on the menu bar and, so long as the user holds down the button, highlights menu choices as he or she moves the pointer over them. When the user releases the mouse, the Menu Manager tells your program what choice was made. Your application must then process the choice. (See Chapter 6 for a discussion of how the Menu Manager and your program relate to each other.)

❖ *Pause for a moment:* Figure 3-3 shows the blocks of programming that have been identified to this point. You can see that the program itself is not yet very large. You need to be familiar with only a handful of commands to understand the main event loop of a Macintosh program.

REPEAT
Get Next Event

Disk inserted event?
(Ignore unless uninitialized)

Update event?
(Redraw windows as needed)

Mouse event?
Find Window

Desk accessory?
(Call System Click)

Menu bar?
(Call Menu Select)

Other events
(To be discussed)

UNTIL USER QUITS

Figure 3-3
A partial skeleton of the main event loop

An application window

If the mouse is pressed in a window that is created and managed by your program, your next task is to find out which part of the window the user wants to manipulate. Figure 3-4 shows the parts of a window. Depending on which one of them is selected by the user, your program takes different steps to process the input.

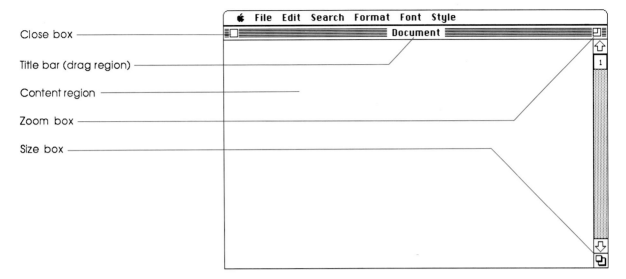

Close box

Title bar (drag region)

Content region

Zoom box

Size box

Figure 3-4
The parts of a Macintosh window

The first thing your program should do is call the Window Manager routine `SelectWindow`. This routine brings the window to the top of the desktop display if it is not already there. To accomplish this, the routine takes the following steps, which are transparent to your program:

1. Unhighlight the previously active window.

2. Bring the selected window in front of all the other windows.

3. Highlight the window that is now active.

4. Generate appropriate activate events as described above.

Outside the content area of the window: If the mouse is pressed in the frontmost window but outside the work area of the window, it can be in any of five places: the title bar, the size box, the close box, a scroll bar, or the zoom box.

With these application window routines added, the main event loop looks like Figure 3-5. Obviously, a great deal of this loop involves managing routines that are not directly related to your application. This overhead programming has been seen by some as a hindrance to Macintosh program development. As much as two-thirds of the application's code—depending, of course, on the nature of the application and its complexity—can be taken up with this overhead programming.

```
REPEAT
Get Next Event
     Disk inserted event?

     Update event?

     Mouse event?
     Find Window

          Application window?

          Go-away region?
          (Call Track Go Away)

          Drag region?
          (Call Drag Window)

          Grow region?
          (Call Grow Window)

          Zoom region?
          (Call Zoom Window)

          Content region?
          (Handle as application desires)

     Key down event?

     Active event?

     Update event?

UNTIL DONE
```

Figure 3-5
A main event loop with the window routines

At the same time, the overhead programming is not difficult. For the most part, it is handled by the Macintosh.

By using a modular application program like MacApp (see Chapter 8), you can avoid having to program the overhead routines even to the extent described in this chapter. This is possible because the Macintosh user interface is sufficiently standardized to permit a predefined way of dealing with such events.

More about events

There is a great deal more power and complexity to the Event Manager than you need to know to create useable Macintosh programs. To give you a glimpse of this power, this section discusses the event queue and event masks. The objective is not to explore these aspects in depth but to convey some of the potential for control of an event-driven program.

The event queue

As events occur in the system, they are placed on the **event queue,** a 20-item list that is stored in priority order. Events stay in the queue until they are processed by `GetNextEvent` calls (or other routines) or until the queue gets full. When the queue is filled with events, a new event will replace one in the queue, with lowest priority and oldest events being eliminated first.

Two types of events are never placed in the event queue: activate and update events are intercepted by the Event Manager and processed automatically. Before checking the event queue in response to a `GetNextEvent` call, the Event Manager checks to see if any activate events are pending. If so, it processes these events before accessing the event queue. The system automatically looks for update events when no other kind of event is going on.

Event masking

A **mask** can be thought of as a kind of filter through which information is passed to see if it fits a predetermined pattern. If it does, it is allowed to pass. If it does not fit the pattern, it is rejected or ignored.

Whenever you use the `GetNextEvent` call, you can optionally supply an event mask that tells the Event Manager the type(s) of events in which you are interested. Each type of event has a numeric value associated with it, as shown in Table 3-1. (Table 3-1 does not show all the types of masks available in the Event Manager, just the ones that are important enough that you should be aware of them now.) Notice that there are four application-definable masks at the high end of the numeric ranges defined in Table 3-1.

Table 3-1
Event masks and their numeric values

Events to mask	Numeric value
Mouse-down	2
Mouse-up	4
Key pressed	8
Key held down (auto)	32
Update	64
Disk inserted	128
Activate	256
Application-defined	4096, 8192, 16384, -32768

Generally speaking, however, you will probably want to leave the event mask alone and permit the system to notify your program of all kinds of events rather than focusing on any one type or group of types.

Note, too, that the event mask doesn't prevent events from being placed in the event queue. It only determines which kinds of events the Event Manager will report to you from the queue when a GetNextEvent is received. Thus, you can't use the event mask to keep the event queue from reaching its 20-event maximum.

A note about errors

Because this chapter is the first to deal with specific Toolbox routines, it is a good place to insert an important observation. Virtually all Toolbox calls result in a return value of some sort. If the routine you call can produce an error condition, the return value may be zero (noErr in Macintosh documentation) or nonzero. If it's nonzero, you must deal with it before proceeding.

It is almost impossible to exaggerate the importance of this advice. If you fail to check for error conditions simply because you don't see any way a particular call in your application could produce an error, a crash can result. The amount of overhead involved in checking the return value to be sure it is nonzero is negligible compared with the loss of programming time you'll experience if an error occurs and you haven't checked for it.

Chapter 4

Memory Management

Memory management on the Macintosh poses one of the most interesting paradoxes of the system. It is at once one of the simplest to use collections of ideas in the Macintosh software architecture and one of the most often misunderstood. More misleading mythology has built up around the Memory Manager than any other manager or package in the system.

This chapter explains the Macintosh Memory Manager. It discusses how the Memory Manager works, what you must do for your programs to interact correctly with it, and when and how objects stored in the Macintosh's memory can be relocated by the Memory Manager.

Before reading this chapter, you might want to read the chapter "Macintosh Memory" in *Technical Introduction to the Macintosh Family*. It contains a thorough discussion of how memory on the Macintosh is organized, which this chapter touches on only lightly.

How memory is organized

Figure 4-1 is a generalized Macintosh memory map. It does not show precise memory locations because those addresses vary depending on the Macintosh model and configuration options. More importantly, you and your application need not know any absolute memory addresses.

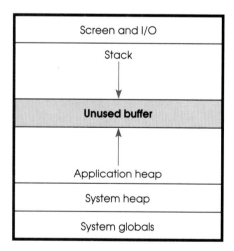

Figure 4-1
A simplified Macintosh memory map

The stack starts near the top of high memory and grows down, while the application heap grows from its assigned starting location up toward high memory. A buffer is automatically created between them. The application heap grows to a fixed limit. However, you must monitor the stack to ensure that collision with the application heap does not occur.

The system globals area contains values needed by all applications running in the environment. Typically, your program has little direct interaction with this information. Any needed activity is handled transparently by the development system you use.

Memory and the parking garage

The Memory Manager on the Macintosh resembles an attended parking garage in some interesting ways. By contrast, the more traditional methods of memory management used on other microcomputers more closely resemble a self-parking garage.

In a self-parking garage, you drive your car to a level where you can find a space. Then you must make a careful note of where your car is parked. Sometimes, the parking garage labels pillars and places signs where you can see them so that you can identify with something close to a memory address. Other times, you have to look around and remember landmarks, location of the car relative to the elevators, and other, less precise memory-joggers to help you recall where your car is.

When you return to get your car, you must remember where it is parked. You must also remember to keep track of the ticket.

In a valet parking garage, you simply drive your car to the point where the attendant takes over. You leave your car and keys in the control of the attendant, who gives you a numbered ticket that corresponds to one he puts on your car for identification. The attendant may park your car on the third level near the elevators or on the fifth floor at the opposite end from the elevator. You don't know and you need not concern yourself with the issue. During the day, the attendant may need to move your car to deliver other cars to their owners or to make room for new ones coming into the lot. You still don't care.

All you really need to know is that when you come back to pick up
your car, the parking lot attendant finds it, starts it, and delivers it
to you in return for payment.

In a conventional microcomputer system, you must know where
your program is storing things it needs. You must be in control.
You are using a self-parking garage and if you forget your ticket or
lose track of where you put something in memory, you are going
to be in serious trouble.

On the Macintosh, though, you simply let the Memory Manager
play the role of parking lot attendant. You tell the Memory
Manager to store something for you, and it gives you the memory
equivalent of a numbered ticket. No matter where or how many
times the Memory Manager cum parking lot valet may relocate
your object to make room for others while your program is
running, you can always return the numbered ticket to the
Memory Manager and expect the data to be returned to you.

As the chapter develops, these analogies will become even
clearer. For now, the important idea to remember is that you
don't have to concern yourself much with what is happening with
the Memory Manager. You can concentrate on problem-solving
rather than on memory-tracking. The idea takes some getting used
to, but it results in far more efficient use of your time.

The elements of Macintosh memory

The Memory Manager consists of several elements, all grouped
together into one manager that keeps track of where things are in
memory and how they can be retrieved or updated as needed.
The five basic objects with which the Memory Manager must deal,
regardless of the program it is running, are

☐ pointers

☐ handles

☐ blocks

☐ the stack

☐ heaps

In some ways, these terms are defined similarly to what you may be accustomed to in conventional computers. More precise definitions begin in the following paragraphs but are expanded as the chapter develops the basic ideas of Macintosh memory management.

Pointers

A pointer is probably not new to you, particularly if you have programmed in C or Pascal. In the Macintosh, a pointer is nearly identical to those kinds of pointers. A **pointer** is an address that tells your program where to find a particular block in memory. Usually, of course, a pointer is stored in a variable that you use to reference the block of memory.

Pointers, then, point directly at the object and are associated with nonrelocatable blocks. This is in direct contrast with handles.

Handles

Handles are pointers to pointers. A handle stores the address where a pointer to a block of memory can be found. Like a pointer, a handle is usually a variable your program uses. When your program is using handles, however, it must use them to locate pointers, which in turn must be used to reference the actual blocks of memory. This is the essence of relocatable blocks.

Blocks

Information stored in the Macintosh's memory by your program is viewed by the Memory Manager as composed of **blocks.** The Memory Manager neither knows nor cares what is stored in those blocks. Your program may use a block for each object it stores in memory, or it may group objects into blocks of related information. To the Memory Manager, all blocks are the same. Discussions of the Memory Manager and its operations almost always talk about locating blocks in memory rather than finding objects there.

The stack

The **stack** on the Macintosh is similar in many ways to that on other microcomputer systems. It starts near the top of high memory and grows down. Stack management is handled automatically by the Memory Manager for all practical purposes. A key difference between the Macintosh stack and other microcomputer stacks is that data is not allocated on the stack on the Macintosh. Data allocation takes place on the heap.

Heaps

There are always at least two **heaps** in the Macintosh's memory when a program is running. The **system heap** is used by the Macintosh Operating System and by Toolbox calls to allocate data needed by the system. (See "System Use of Memory" later in this chapter.) The **application heap** is the portion of memory set aside for your application to allocate data. But, there are times when the system will indirectly allocate memory in this heap on behalf of your application.

This model differs from the traditional microcomputer memory management approach in which only the user's application manipulates the contents of the heap.

Basic memory management

Macintosh memory management is essentially quite simple. When your program needs some memory, it decides whether to use a relocatable or nonrelocatable block, calls the appropriate routine, checks the return code to be sure the memory allocation was successful, and then continues with its processing. When it needs to access an object stored in a block of memory, it does so by **dereferencing** the handle or pointer and retrieving the data. When it no longer needs the memory, it disposes of it.

Aside from the question of relocatable and nonrelocatable blocks, Macintosh memory management differs little from traditional computer memory management. But relocatable blocks are such an important concept in the Macintosh that they deserve further attention.

Relocatable and nonrelocatable blocks

The *relocatability* of a block refers to the freedom with which the Memory Manager can manipulate blocks of storage when it is asked to allocate additional space. Relocatable objects can be moved freely by the Memory Manager when it must do so. Nonrelocatable blocks are sacrosanct; they will not move.

Your program manages relocatable blocks of memory using handles and nonrelocatable blocks using pointers.

Your program must be concerned with the manipulation of these two types of memory blocks because of memory **fragmentation.** This fragmentation, in turn, comes about because the Memory Manager frequently moves relocatable blocks in memory to allocate new space as it is needed.

It is important to note, however, that these blocks are only moved at specific, well-known times, and that you determine whether any given block of memory is relocatable.

Moving blocks in memory

The Memory Manager relocates blocks of memory that your program has allocated only when

☐ the blocks are relocatable

☐ a need for more memory arises

☐ a block of sufficient size is not immediately available without moving one or more blocks of memory.

On the surface, it would appear that blocks of memory arc relocated only when your program requests additional memory and the above circumstances are present. But that is not quite true. Many Toolbox calls made directly or indirectly by your program also require memory allocation. This need for additional memory that is not explicitly and directly requested by your program makes Macintosh memory management at once important and elegant.

When the Memory Manager does relocate a block of space, it places the beginning address of the new block at the address to which that block's handle points. Figure 4-2 depicts the process.

Before move

	Address	Contents
Block 1	$2947C	
Pointer	$229C0	$2947C
Handle	$D94AE	$229C0

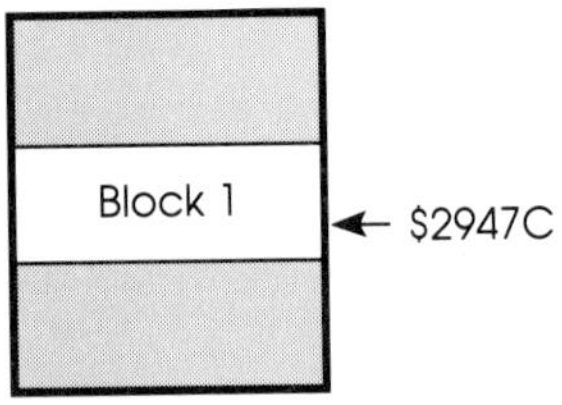

Block 1 ← $2947C

After move

	Address	Contents
Block 1	$22A00	
Pointer	$229C0	$22A00
Handle	$D94AE	$229C0

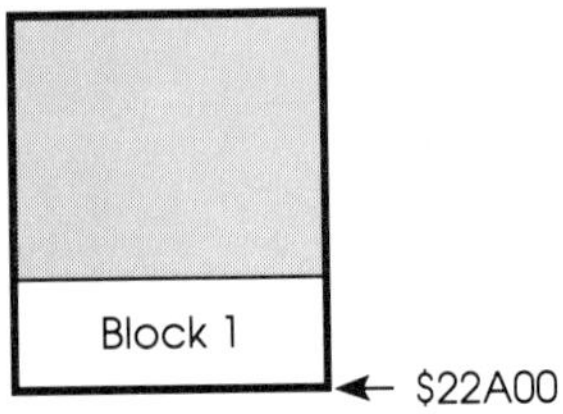

Block 1 ← $22A00

Figure 4-2
Memory block relocation

Before BLOCK1 in Figure 4-2 is relocated by the Memory Manager, it begins at address $2947C. The pointer to it is stored at $229C0 and contains the block's starting address of $2947C. The handle contains the address of the pointer, $229C0. After the block is relocated, notice that although the *contents* of the pointer have changed to reflect the new starting address of BLOCK1, the *address* of the pointer has not changed. The handle still points to the pointer, which still points to the block, even though the Memory Manager has relocated the block. This means, among other things, that the handle can still obtain the data in the memory block called BLOCK1.

To return to the parking lot analogy, the handle is similar to the ticket the attendant gives you when you give him your car. The ticket contains a number. By keeping track of where the car with that numbered tag is parked, the attendant can retrieve your car when you need it even if he's moved it and even if you can't describe it very well. (Remember, the Memory Manager doesn't know or care what is stored in the block.)

Fragmentation

So long as the parking lot attendant has the keys to everyone's car and control over where they are parked, he can keep the parking lot as full as possible and usually manage to find place for yet another car when space is needed. Lock the cars and put everyone in charge of moving their own car and chaos will result. There might be a space available for a sleek new sports car that just pulled into the driveway, but if access to that space is blocked by someone who's locked his car, the space is unusable.

This is precisely what happens when you design programs that include nonrelocatable blocks. The Memory Manager cannot move those objects, so when it needs to allocate new space for a newly created block, it may be unable to do so. The result is equivalent to having run out of memory, even though there may be huge chunks of it lying around unused.

There are two ways a block of memory can become nonrelocatable. You can define it as such when you create it or you can lock a relocatable block temporarily (a practice that is discouraged).

Unlike the stack, the application heap is not a LIFO (last in, first out) area of memory. If you allocate space for four nonrelocatable objects in the heap (see Figure 4-3) and then your program no longer needs one of them and releases it, the vacated space is simply marked as free by the Memory Manager.

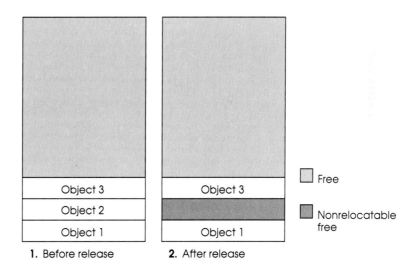

1. Before release   **2.** After release

Figure 4-3
The beginning of heap fragmentation

When your program allocates more heap space for another object (see Figure 4-4), the Memory Manager must find a location that contains sufficient contiguous bytes to store the object. If the object is even slightly too large to fit into the space recently vacated by another object, the old vacancy remains and new space must be allocated.

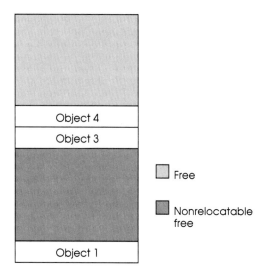

Figure 4-4
Allocating new space

It is not difficult to imagine what the heap looks like after a program of any complexity allocates and removes a number of nonrelocatable objects from the application heap. Figure 4-5, while perhaps a bit exaggerated, depicts the problem you'd be facing. It is essential that your program allow the Memory Manager to manage the application heap. That is why it makes sense to make objects relocatable unless there is a compelling reason not to do so.

With relocatable blocks in the application heap, the Memory Manager can move blocks around to gain contiguous free space for a new object to be created and stored.

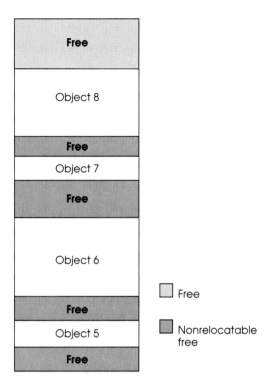

Figure 4-5
A badly fragmented heap

Obtaining and releasing memory blocks

There are two basic calls your programs will use to obtain memory. A call to NewHandle returns a handle to a relocatable block of memory. Similarly, a call to NewPtr returns a pointer to a nonrelocatable block of memory. Each of these calls takes one argument, the size of the block of memory to be allocated.

Of course, after either of these calls is carried out, your program should check the return value. If the handle or pointer returned by the call is Nil, then the attempt to allocate the memory has failed and your program must react accordingly.

When your program is finished using a particular block it has allocated, it calls the appropriate routine. DisposHandle releases memory allocated to a relocatable object, and DisposPtr deallocates memory assigned to a nonrelocatable block.

It is important that you only dispose of memory blocks that your program allocates directly.

Memory reorganization

Clearly, the Macintosh Memory Manager works best when it has maximum freedom. When nonrelocatable blocks are kept to a minimum, the Memory Manager has a better chance of finding memory blocks when they are needed, even if they are quite large. You, as a programmer, do not need to concern yourself with the details of how and when the Memory Manager relocates things or where it puts them. As you have seen, the relocation is transparent to your program.

Still, it is useful in understanding the Macintosh to have a grasp of how it decides what to relocate.

When memory is needed, the Macintosh moves all relocatable blocks as low in the application heap as it can. If this process does not result in a space large enough for the new or enlarged object, it purges blocks as permitted. These purgeable blocks may consist of resources, which are discussed in greater detail in Chapter 2. Following this step, the Memory Manager may move some more relocatable objects. Once any purgeable resources are released, the Memory Manager allocates the new space. If it still cannot find a large enough contiguous space, it can move more relocatable objects, because the purge of resources may have freed up additional space.

After trying all of those options, if the Memory Manager still cannot allocate the memory needed, it returns a Nil handle or pointer to the application that made the call.

System use of memory

In the Macintosh programming world, your application shares memory with the system. A wide variety of Toolbox routines can allocate memory on the application heap; these are listed in *Inside Macintosh*. The important point to remember about the system's use of memory is that it makes it necessary for you to monitor heap usage even when your application has not allocated any new memory since you last used the heap.

For example, if your program checks on how much memory is available and gets a value indicating that 278,589 bytes are available in the application heap, that figure may or may not be the same 10 minutes later. This is true even if between the time you got that answer and the time you are about to rely on it, your program has done nothing directly to request more memory. In fact, even if your program has done nothing *indirectly* to request new memory, it may not be correct. Why? Because Macintosh users can call desk accessories, among other good reasons.

If your program is whizzing merrily along and the user decides to load a new font, read in another file to look up something, or do any one of a number of other things that affect memory, your program is probably not going to be aware of the user's actions. Yet they clearly have an impact on memory. A font, for example, can occupy several thousand bytes of memory, and that memory is taken from the application heap.

The lesson is simple. Check memory before you attempt to allocate any. Then allocate it. Then check to be sure the memory was allocated properly. Then pretend you don't know how much memory is left (because you don't).

Your program and the segment loader

Your program code is a resource, and as a result, it is loaded into memory when it is needed. (Chapter 6 discusses the Resource Manager, which is in charge of such memory manipulation.)

Many Macintosh development systems limit code segments to 32K. This and the modular nature of efficient Macintosh programming mean that almost all nontrivial Macintosh programs are divided into segments.

Why segment your code?

There are at least two good reasons for segmenting your Macintosh programs:

□ The general 32K limit on the size of a single code segment necessitates such a strategy. This is true particularly in view of the user interface management you do in the main event loop.

□ Segmenting code makes for good memory management and more efficient program execution.

Three classes of programs

From a memory and segmentation perspective, programs can be thought of as falling into three categories:

□ Programs that are smaller than 32K. These are often stored as a single segment. Segmentation is not an issue.

□ Programs that are larger than 32K but smaller than the application heap. In these cases, segmentation is useful primarily because you must consider the possibility that the user will need memory that is unrelated to your program (or only peripherally related). So you will probably segment such programs, loading the segments when needed and unloading them when they are not in use. For example, you might have segments that initialize variables and data structures. Another segment might handle printing-related functions. After the program has initialized and when printing is complete, you can unload these segments (see "Unloading Segments" later in this chapter).

□ Programs that are larger than the application heap. These programs must be segments or they simply will not run. Unloading segments that are no longer needed moves from a polite maneuver to a mandatory design technique.

Deciding on the segments' contents

The key thing to keep in mind when deciding which of your programs' routines to group together into a segment is that the Macintosh system loads into memory all of the routines in a segment whenever you use any one of the routines in that segment. This leads logically to the fundamental rule of segmentation:

Rule   Group related routines together into segments.

If, for example, your code includes a set of routines that key off a specific menu resource, and if those routines are subject to being called by the user's interaction with the menu bar, put all of those routines into one segment. If you don't, the user may spend a lot of time waiting for disk access while the segments containing the needed code are loaded before the program can continue.

Fundamentally, the principles involved in making segmentation decisions in your Macintosh applications are identical to those involved in top-down, structured programming. Keep like things together so they can work together.

Trade-offs in segmentation decisions

Some routines don't fall neatly into either the main event loop or grouped collections of related procedures. In those cases, you have to decide if you want to form many small, individual segments or incorporate them into the main segment, which is always in memory.

If you put too many small routines into individual segments, program execution suffers. Disk accesses (among the slowest activities in any program on any machine) may become excessive.

But putting too much code into memory at one time in the main segment results in inefficient use of memory.

The best advice is probably to start by putting small, frequently needed routines into the main segment along with the main event loop, and everything else into as many segments as necessary and logical for grouping related functions. Then as you polish and debug your program, keep an eye on execution times, load times, pauses in execution for disk I/O, and the like, and adjust accordingly. The process is necessarily dynamic.

The main segment

The main segment of your program—known technically as CODE segment 1—is loaded into memory when your application starts and is never purged or unlocked as long as the program is executing. This segment is where the main event loop and frequently needed small routines are generally stored. Do not take this to imply, however, that you can't have any number of segments that are never purged or unlocked while your program is executing. The main segment is not unique in this respect, but it is the only one that is *automatically* treated this way.

If you follow recommended programming practices and create your Macintosh application as a main event loop that dispatches tasks to other handler routines, this main segment model with other segments loaded and unloaded as needed will make eminent sense.

Loading segments

You need never be concerned with explicitly loading segments. When a segment is needed, the segment loader handles the task transparently.

Unloading segments

Because the Memory Manager has no way to tell when a segment of code can be unloaded, it is incumbent on you to notify the system of this. The simplest way is to call `UnloadSeg` for all of your segments each time you go through the main event loop. This action will not, of course, unload any segments you have marked as nonpurgeable, including the main code segment. This approach is often sufficient, but it is not essential that you do this if there are reasons to avoid it.

`UnloadSeg` does not, as its name implies, actually unload the segment. Instead, it unlocks it and makes it purgeable, permitting the Memory Manager to purge it or relocate the space it occupies if it needs to do so to gain some space in the application heap, as discussed earlier.

Out-of-memory conditions

You can't be around Macintosh programming very long before you encounter a discussion of the out-of-memory conditions that sometimes arise during program development.

What causes memory to "disappear"?

There are three primary causes of out-of-memory conditions:

- □ overzealous use of nonrelocatable blocks
- □ desk accessories
- □ the system's use of memory

Nonrelocatable blocks

It is important enough to be worth stressing once again that you should only create nonrelocatable blocks when it's essential.

Fragmentation of the heap can cause memory to be unavailable when it's needed even if the total amount of space available is more than adequate.

Desk accessories

Any well-designed Macintosh application must be aware of desk accessories.

Users expect desk accessories to be available whenever they are doing anything on a Macintosh. Most desk accessories require the use of some of the application heap. So your program can be humming along nicely, managing its memory and keeping things under control when all of a sudden things become unruly because a user calls the calculator. Your program must take into account that it is likely users will do such things and that the desk accessories they invoke will require application heap space. There is no way to anticipate how many desk accessories requiring how much memory may be activated by the user. Desk accessories are only opened through your program, however, so you can at least manage the impact such actions have on memory.

The system's use of memory

Perhaps the most troublesome source of memory problems on the Macintosh is the fact that Toolbox routines call other Toolbox routines, which in turn can call still other Toolbox routines. The Grand Funnel in Chapter 1 made this seemingly unpredictable operation of the Macintosh clear. As a result, you need to be particularly cognizant of what is happening "beneath" your application. If your routines use Toolbox calls that can have a direct impact on memory usage, the application must take this into account.

The Dialog Manager, for example, calls the Window Manager. A Dialog Manager call therefore has a potential impact on memory at least as great as that of creating a new window, even though this indirect impact is not necessarily obvious.

Two strategies for handling out-of-memory conditions

If available memory gets sufficiently low, your program cannot allocate the space needed to post a message telling the user to save documents, close windows, shut down, or otherwise gracefully exit from the program. Yet, a program that simply crashes when memory runs low or is exhausted will not win friends in the user community.

Memory management is one of the issues a Macintosh application programmer must take into account early in the design process and keep in mind throughout the development. What is often an afterthought or even a point of no concern in other kinds of microcomputer programming becomes a major design consideration in the Macintosh.

At least two possible strategies have been identified for anticipating out-of-memory conditions and dealing with them in ways users will find helpful. These strategies may be conveniently labeled as follows:

□ preflighting memory allocation
□ reserved heap space allocation

Preflighting

Preflighting is the process of having your application allocate the space a Toolbox call is about to seek. If the allocation succeeds, then the Toolbox also succeeds. At that point, have your program free the memory and call the Toolbox routine. If an out-of-memory condition is detected by your application, you can take appropriate action.

Reserved heap space

Another approach is to allocate a block of arbitrary size that will be available to deal with out-of-memory conditions. If a memory error is encountered during your program's execution, you can free some arbitrary portion of this specially reserved area and notify the user that space is running low. This permits the user to save documents, close windows, or take other steps that minimize the impact of a memory shortage.

The process can be repeated once or twice, each time allocating a smaller amount of memory and sending the user a more strongly worded warning.

Chapter 5

Display and Graphics Routines

This chapter looks at one of the most obvious and intriguing features of the Macintosh family of computers: their visually oriented display. Even a person who doesn't use computers can immediately tell a Macintosh application by the extensive use of graphics, fonts, and windows on the screen. Other microcomputer environments are now beginning to emulate the Macintosh "look" because of the ease of use it offers.

An obvious advantage

At heart, the Macintosh is a graphics machine. This difference by itself would be enough to make it a radical departure from the last generation's computers. The advantages of it are becoming obvious to users.

But although the advantages are obvious, the intricacies and operation of the graphics routines are anything but obvious. There's a great deal of power and depth in the QuickDraw and Color QuickDraw routines, and these libraries account for a larger share of the Toolbox than any other single manager or package.

Fortunately, there is some commonality among calls that makes learning what they do and how they do it much easier than might appear to be the case at first glance.

Programmers coming from nongraphics microcomputer environments often look at the Macintosh graphics capabilities and wonder if they can create programs that run acceptably fast with all the calculation and screen manipulation involved. The beauty of QuickDraw is that it is not only relatively easy to use, but also amazingly fast. If you've designed applications that required you to plot and draw circles using traditional methods, you are going to find QuickDraw's `frameOval` call a joy to use.

Everything is in graphics

The most important idea to garner from this chapter is that in the Macintosh, *everything is done in graphics*. If it's displayed on the screen or sent to the printer, it involves graphics routines that are part of the extensive QuickDraw and Color QuickDraw repertoire. It is obvious that shapes like circles, ovals, rectangles, and lines that show up in windows designed to display charts and pictures are graphic in nature. But the rectangle that makes up the window is also created using QuickDraw routines. So are the scroll bars, the size box, the close box, the zoom box, and a great deal of other window-related objects. For that matter, even the text displayed is a graphic object.

Icons are graphic images, of course, but so are menus, so is text, and so are radio buttons and check boxes, the heart of the dialog boxes with which even the most casual Macintosh user is familiar.

Not only is everything on the Macintosh screen handled with graphics, but so is anything that is sent to the printer. Printing is a simple matter of sending a graphic image to someplace other than the screen.

QuickDraw and Color QuickDraw routines are the foundation of many other managers and routines, at least in terms of what the user sees and interacts with as he or she uses Macintosh applications.

A world of graphics in a library

The built-in QuickDraw routines in the Macintosh Toolbox are very much like libraries of routines you might have purchased separately for more conventional microcomputers.

Need to plot a circle as part of a complex graph? It's not necessary to plot each individual point and draw it. Just call the appropriate QuickDraw routine and pass the screen location and size. The circle is calculated and plotted for you automatically, to say nothing of quickly. The same is true of the other shapes QuickDraw and Color QuickDraw handle: rectangles, round-cornered rectangles, arcs, wedges, and polygons.

For complex graphic compositions, you can use the QuickDraw picture routines. These permit you to store a script of connected QuickDraw calls that can later be recalled and played back. The result is virtually instant display of such graphic images.

A quick look at QuickDraw

All display and printing routines in the Macintosh use **bit-mapped graphics.** This term refers to the process of mapping, or making connections between, bits stored in memory and pixels displayed on the screen. Each bit in memory representing a portion of a graphic image is a 1 or a 0 in the classic Macintosh with a monochrome display. On the Macintosh II, things are understandably more complex because each screen location contains more than simple "on-off" information, but the basic QuickDraw routines change only minimally.

On all models of Macintosh, drawing takes place in a **graphics port,** often referred to as a *grafPort.* A graphics port is a complete drawing environment that contains the data QuickDraw and Color QuickDraw need to create and manipulate bit or pixel images. Many programs create and manage more than one graphics port, each containing different information about the drawing environment.

The most important shape in QuickDraw's world is the rectangle. Not only are windows, scroll bars, and other controls rectangles, but the screen is as well. In addition, even ovals (and their special case, circles) are defined in terms of the rectangles they occupy. In fact, even bit maps in Macintosh memory are defined in terms of a **boundary rectangle** that gives dimension to the image.

QuickDraw routines allow you to create lines, shapes, patterns with which to draw lines and fill shapes (including cursors), fonts, and icons.

The discussion in this chapter assumes you have a fundamental grasp of QuickDraw and Color QuickDraw. If you feel uncomfortable with any of the ideas presented here or want more background before proceeding, read *Technical Introduction to the Macintosh Family.*

"When you get ready to program a Macintosh, study QuickDraw first. You really have to learn it. Not only will you use its routines a lot, but it's a great example of how to program the Macintosh."

Eric Zocher,
Silicon Beach Software

The QuickDraw programming model

Before you can carry out any QuickDraw operations in an application, you must initialize its routines using a call to `InitGraf`. It is dangerous to call `InitGraf` more than once in a session, so desk accessories should never call it. The call to `InitGraf` is the same whether you are using QuickDraw or Color QuickDraw calls in the program.

❖ *Note:* In some high-level language implementations, a reference to an include file or an external unit automatically initializes QuickDraw. The issue is not so much the specific call but that the initialization must take place once and only once.

With QuickDraw initialized, you are ready to draw something into a graphics port. Good programming practice dictates that this take place in four steps, as shown in Figure 5-1.

Initialize QuickDraw
Open a window for drawing

- **Drawing text?**
  - Set font characteristics
  - Draw the text
- **Drawing a line?**
  - Set pen characteristics
  - Line To (from point to point)
- **Drawing a shape?**
  - Set pen characteristics
  - Frame appropriate shape
  - Fill if requested

Figure 5-1
The basic structure of a QuickDraw routine

This skeleton approach to QuickDraw programming ensures that the proper port is current before your program begins drawing. The `GetPort` routine permits your program to save the port that was active before the drawing routine was called, and the `SetPort` routine sets up the right current port in which your program can draw. The drawing routines then take care of presenting whatever information you wish in the current graphics port. After the drawing, you restore the old graphics port with another `SetPort` call to the old port.

You may be tempted to shortcut this approach by not keeping track of which port is current and which old port is being deactivated by the QuickDraw calls. Even if your program uses only one graphics port, however, this is not good Macintosh programming practice. A desk accessory could create another port and you could find your program's output inadvertently modifying its contents. The overhead cost of being safe is minimal.

❖ *Note:* The misuse of `SetPort` is one of the most common sources of errors in Macintosh programs.

Bits and pixels, maps and images

Data that translates directly into screen images is stored in the form of bit images and bit maps on the classic Macintosh and pixel images and pixel maps on the Macintosh SE and Macintosh II. The differences are somewhat subtle but important. This section looks briefly at these structures and how they are used. More information can be found in Volumes I and V of *Inside Macintosh.*

Bit images

A **bit image** is a collection of bits in memory laid out like a rectangle. It can be arbitrarily large. A bit image can be thought of as beginning a collection of contiguous memory locations containing words. Bit 15 of the lowest numbered word is on the left, and bit 0 of the highest numbered word is on the right. This vector of bytes is then converted into a rectilinear structure like that shown in Figure 5-2. The dark vertical lines represent word boundaries. The number of bytes in each row of the image is referred to as the bit image's *row width*. A bit image can be any length that is an even multiple of the row width.

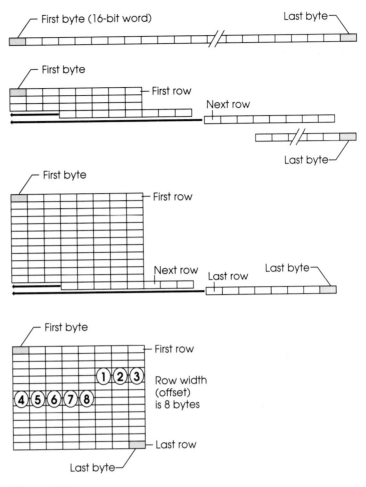

Figure 5-2
A bit image

Pixel images

A **pixel image** is used exactly the same way on the newer Macintosh systems as the bit image is on the earlier ones. The only difference is that a pixel image has depth. A bit image can be thought of as a one-bit-deep pixel image. A pixel image typically is one to eight bits deep. The deeper the pixel image, the more colors can be displayed at a time on the screen. The trade-off is that more colors mean longer screen redrawing times. Figure 5-3 shows a pixel image.

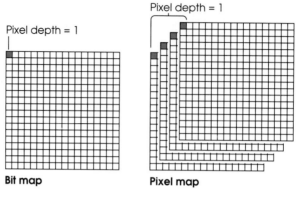

Pixel depth = 1

Pixel depth = 1

Bit map

Pixel map

Figure 5-3
A pixel image

Bit maps

The classic Macintosh keeps track of bit images and where they should be displayed on the screen by means of a data structure called a **bit map.** This structure contains a pointer to the bit image, an integer defining the row width of the image, and the coordinates of the boundary rectangle within which the bit image is to be displayed. The boundary rectangle defines the dimensions and the coordinate system for the bit map. Coordinate systems are covered later in this chapter.

All drawing takes place in the bit map and is transferred to the screen by built-in routines that are invisible to your program.

Pixel maps

As you would expect, the **pixel map** used in the color world of Macintosh is more complex than the bit map of monochrome displays. A pixel map has the same 3 fields as a bit map but adds 12 new fields. These additional fields deal with color and with the fact that on the newer Macintosh systems, displays other than the built-in monochrome monitor of the earlier Macintosh may be used. This condition makes it necessary to store resolution data.

As with bit maps, the newer Macintosh systems do all of their drawing in the pixel map and then translate that into a screen display by processes that are invisible to your program.

Graphics ports

Although we often speak and think of graphics ports as if they were screen images, technically they are data structures stored in your application heap. Each graphics port has a separate data structure defining all of its characteristics. Switching from one graphics port to another is as simple and fast as using `GetPort` to remember the one you are leaving and `SetPort` to cause subsequent output to be sent to the new port.

Although graphics ports are the structures upon which a program builds the windows, it is important not to confuse graphics ports with windows. Any single window may contain many graphics ports. Similarly, a single graphics port may span multiple windows, though programs are not generally designed this way.

What's in a graphics port's record?

Figure 5-4 shows the data structure of a record of type grafPort. Note that it can be divided into eight groups of related fields. At the outset, however, you should understand that your application will typically never directly modify any of the fields in this record. Modification takes place by calls to appropriate QuickDraw routines as described later in the chapter. QuickDraw owns this data structure, and it is not good form for your program to write directly to it.

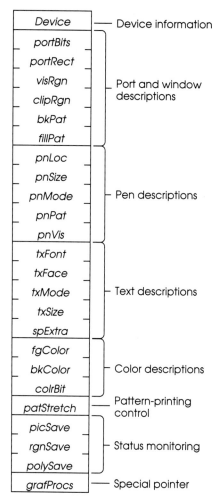

| Device | — Device information |

Figure 5-4
The structure of a graphics port record

Device information

The first field is used by the Font Manager to tweak the display of characters for the most pleasing output, depending on whether the device is the Macintosh monochrome screen, a printer, or a color video monitor. This field usually contains a 0, which is the value that produces the best screen output. If your program's output is to be routed to a device other than the screen, the field should be programmed to contain that device's ID number.

Port and window descriptions

The next six fields in the grafPort data record provide information about the port itself and the window associated with the port. The first, portBits, is a pointer to the area in memory where the bit image to be used by the graphics port is stored. The next, portRect, usually defines the area where data will actually be displayed. All drawing takes place inside this rectangle.

How much of a bit image's display is visible on the screen is controlled by the values in the next two fields. The visRgn field stores a handle to the visible region of the display. (Regions are explained under "QuickDrawing.") This area is one your program normally ignores. Its management is automatic. When windows overlap, this field makes it possible for your program to write even in a partially hidden window without the image overflowing onto the front window. Your program does, however, manage the clipRgn field. You can use this field to limit arbitrarily how much of the image being generated the user sees. For example, you can draw a circle within a graphics port where the clipRgn field is set so that the user only sees a half-circle.

The final two fields in this part of the record are used by some QuickDraw routines. The first, bkPat, is the background pattern that is used when an area is erased. The second, fillPat, is a fill pattern used by Macintosh to fill an area. (Patterns are discussed later under "QuickDrawing.")

Pen description

The next five fields define the pen used for drawing all lines, whether the lines are drawn using line-drawing tools or are part of a graphic image such as a shape or picture created in other ways. Figure 5-5 shows the QuickDraw pen and its four main characteristics.

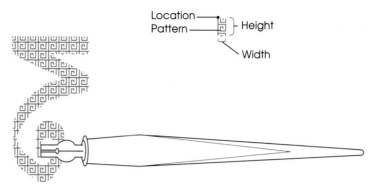

Figure 5-5
A graphics pen

First among these fields is pnLoc, which is the coordinate position of the upper left corner of the pen.

The pen's size is given in the form of two pixel counts. The first is the pen's width and the second is its height. Normally, the pen is 1 pixel by 1 pixel, but you can set any value from 0 to 30,000 in either or both values. The value is stored as if it were an addressed point (x,y coordinate), but it is not used that way. That is just a convenient data structure for the program to use.

A graphics pen can draw using any defined pattern. It need not be a "black ink" line. The pnPat field contains a value that translates into a display pattern. When a pen using any pattern is used to draw over existing representations of bit image data, how it affects those underlying images is determined by the setting of pnMode. One of eight "transfer modes" can be specified by the contents of this field. Depending on this setting, a pixel under a pixel in the new pattern may be left alone, forced to black, forced to white, or inverted from whatever it is at the time. Figure 5-6 depicts how these modes work in combination with underlying objects.

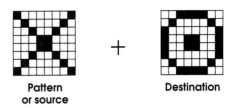

Pattern
or source

Destination

Paint	Overlay	Invert	Erase
patCopy srcCopy	patOr srcOr	patXor srcXor	patBic srcBic
notPatCopy notSrcCopy	notPatOr notSrcOr	notPatXor notSrcXor	notPatBic notSrcBic

Figure 5-6
Pen transfer modes

The last pen information field, pnVis, determines whether the pen's actions are visible. If this field contains a negative value, pen actions do not produce visible results.

Text description

The next five fields describe the text associated with the port.

The font is described as a number in the txFont field. Each font in the Macintosh has a number associated with it. Conflicts between font number should not arise, though they are not automatically prevented by anything in the Macintosh. If two or more fonts have the same font number, only the first one found in the fonts loaded into memory will be accessible. If the txFont field contains a 0, the system font will be used.

Within each font, type may have various sizes and styles. Sizes are expressed in **points** and are stored as an integer in the txSize field. (A point is approximately 1/72 inch.) If the specified font does not have available a font of the size stored in the txSize field, the Font Manager uses scaling algorithms to create one.

Type styles include bold, italic, underlined, outline, shadowed, condensed, extended, and combinations of these (see Figure 5-7). The txStyle field can contain a set of one or more key words that describe these combinations of text styles.

Plain characters

Bold characters

Italic characters

<u>Underlined characters</u>

Outlined characters

Shadowed characters

Condensed characters

Extended characters

Bold Italic characters

Bold Outlined characters

Figure 5-7
Type styles

Like the pnMode field discussed earlier, the txMode field determines how text that appears over other items on the display will appear. Of the eight types of modes available (see Figure 5-6), only srcOr, srcXor, and srcBic should be used for text. Others create unreadable and unpredictable results. (In fact, if you want your programs to be able to display color text clearly and with predictable results, you should only use srcOr as txMode.)

The spExtra field is only used in producing fully justified text. It is beyond the scope of what you need to worry about at this point.

Color description

The next three fields deal with color. Do not confuse these fields with the far more powerful color capabilities included in color graphics ports, which are discussed later in "Color QuickDraw Graphics Ports." These fields are used to permit the classic Macintosh application to produce images in color on output devices that support color, including the ImageWriter® II printer.

The first two of these fields, fgColor and bkColor, define the foreground and background colors to be used in printing. A selection from eight colors is available for each of the two types of color placement (see Table 5-1). The third field, ColrBit, helps the graphics port figure out which layer, or plane, of a graphic image should be printed in the particular color combination.

❖ *Note:* Because colors can be combined to make new colors, they are layered onto the screen, but in a two-dimensional display this is difficult to show. The data structure, however, represents the layers so that a color printing device can produce the best possible output.

Table 5-1
Color selections in monochrome graphics ports

Color	Constant
Black	33
White	30
Red	205
Green	341
Blue	409
Cyan	273
Magenta	137
Yellow	69

Interestingly, if your program uses color printing fields in the graphics port record and then the user prints to an output device that does not handle color, nothing damaging happens. The output is produced correctly.

device
portPix
portVersion
grafVars
chExtra
phLocHFrac
portRect
visRgn
clipRgn
bkPixPat
rgbFgColor
rgbBkColor
pnLoc
pnSize
pnMode
pnPixPat
pnFillPat
pnVis
txFont
txFace
txMode
txSize
spExtra
fgColor
bkColor
colrBit
patStretch
picSave
rgnSave
polySave
grafProcs

Figure 5-8
The structure of a color
graphics port record

Pattern-printing control

The next field, patStretch, is of no particular interest to your program. It controls the way a pattern is altered when it is printed on a hard-copy device rather than displayed on the Macintosh screen.

Status monitoring

The next three fields contain handles to information about pictures (picSave), regions (rgnSave), and polygons (polySave). Your program should not concern itself with these fields except in rare circumstances beyond the scope of this discussion.

Color QuickDraw graphics ports

If you want your program to be able to take advantage of the more powerful color facilities on the Macintosh SE and Macintosh II, you use routines that create color graphics ports, also known as **CGrafPort** data structures. These structures are the same size as the traditional monochrome graphics port records and have many fields in common with those structures. There are, however, ten new fields with which your program will have to deal.

The structure of a color graphics port is shown in Figure 5-8. New fields discussed below are highlighted in the illustration.

The portPix field is a handle that points to the port's pixel map (see "Pixel Maps" earlier in this chapter). The two high-order bits of portVersion are always set to signal a Color QuickDraw port. The rest of the value contains the version number of the Color QuickDraw routines that are in use.

By means of the grafVars field, the color graphics port's data structure was kept the same size. This field contains a handle to the location in memory of some new fields used for new drawing modes implemented in the Macintosh II.

The chExtra field determines the number of pixels by which any character is widened on a line of text to achieve proportional-spaced display and printing. The pnLocHFrac field holds a value that represents the fractional precision of the pen position used when drawing text.

On the newer Macintosh systems, it is possible for the background to contain not only a color but a pattern as well. The background pattern to be used is identified in the bkPixPat field. Similarly, the patterns to be used for the pen is held in pnPixPat and the fill pattern in fillPixPat.

The remaining four new fields determine the background and foreground colors used in displaying and printing information. rgbFgColor and rgbBkColor describe the foreground and background colors, respectively, that have been requested by the program or the user. fgColor and bkColor contain the foreground and background colors actually supplied to the program by the Color Manager. Depending on user requests and the capabilities of the display hardware, these fields can differ from the contents of rgbFgColor and rgbBkColor.

Graphics ports and coordinate systems

Coordinate addresses point to the intersection of mythical grid lines in the coordinate plane, not to an individual bit or pixel. Another way of saying this is that the lines are infinitely thin. They define the outer boundaries within which all the bits or pixels that define a particular shape lie. As a consequence, all elements represented on the coordinate plane are "mathematically pure" and will produce intuitively correct results using integer mathematics.

All information about location or movement is given to QuickDraw in terms of coordinates on a plane. The coordinate system is a two-dimensional grid, as illustrated in Figure 5-9. The origin of this grid, position (0,0), is located at its center, with numbers becoming negative as they move up and left, and positive as they move down and right.

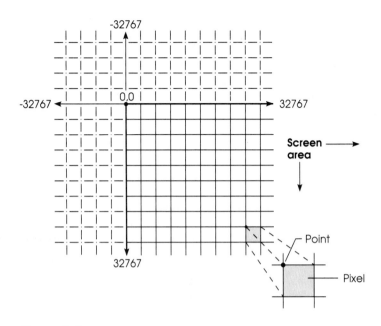

Figure 5-9
QuickDraw's coordinate plane

Local coordinates

Each graphics port has its own **local coordinate system.** Within the port, all fields are expressed in terms of this system and all calculations and actions use it.

When a new graphics port is created, its bit map is set to encompass the entire screen. The upper left corner of the port is set as its origin with coordinates (0,0). Your program may, however, alter the coordinates of this corner of the port with the `SetOrigin` procedure. The corner remains anchored at all times as the reference point for all other coordinate system calls.

If your program must compare or perform calculations on two or more graphics ports, it cannot do so using each port's individual local coordinate system. QuickDraw furnishes routines to convert local coordinates into the **global coordinate system** in which the upper left corner of the port's bit image is set logically to (0,0). Moving between global and local coordinate systems is straightforward. Two procedures are available. The `LocalToGlobal` procedure converts a port from the local coordinate system to the global system. The other procedure, `GlobalToLocal`, reverses the process.

The concepts involved in these coordinate systems and their relationships to each other are important to a thorough understanding of QuickDraw. You should read the QuickDraw chapter in Volume I of *Inside Macintosh* to gain a deeper appreciation for these tools. It is not necessary that you have a thorough understanding of them to make use of the rest of this chapter.

Rectangles

Rectangles play a significant role in the world of QuickDraw. Coordinate systems are rectangular, as are bit and pixel maps. All shape drawing, even that of circles and ovals, takes place inside rectangles.

A rectangle is defined by its upper left and lower right corners, which are given coordinate addresses. QuickDraw provides numerous built-in routines that permit you to manipulate and perform calculations on rectangles.

QuickDrawing

The discussion in this section focuses on the classic Macintosh with monochrome display, but the techniques are also largely applicable to the newer color-capable Macintosh family members. Differences between the two types of Macintosh programming are explained in "Color QuickDraw" later in this chapter.

An outline of a QuickDraw program

Here is a skeleton of the program code that would normally be used in a program to display text or graphics in a window.

```
InitGraf(pointer to the port)

InitWindows

FlushEvents(everyEvent,0)

InitCursor

NewWindow(window-creating information)

SetPort(pointer to the window)

(drawing routines)
```

This fragment is necessarily broad and oversimplified. Notice that graphics must be initialized before they can be used, which is the function of the first command in the list. Next, you perform an `InitWindows` call to initialize the Window Manager. Most of the time, your drawing will take place in a window, so you use the Window Manager to open, track, and handle your graphics ports.

The drawing routines can include any or all of the routines described in this section.

Lines and the QuickDraw pen

The QuickDraw graphics pen has a number of characteristics associated with it. These include a size, a location, a pattern, a transfer mode, and the possibility of being visible or invisible. QuickDraw routines permit you to determine the current state of the pen and alter its traits as needed. With the pen's status established as desired, either of two line-drawing routines can be used.

To find out the current status and location of the pen, you can use `GetPen` or `GetPenState`, depending on how much data you need. `GetPen` tells your program where the pen is located. (Remember, too, that because each graphics port has its own pen associated with it, the pen won't move when you switch ports and then switch back again.) `GetPenState` also allows your program to find out the size, transfer mode, and drawing pattern in addition to its location.

One good use of these two routines is the storage of current pen information so that you can make a temporary change and restore the original pen with little programming overhead.

The size of the pen can be altered with the `PenSize` call and its transfer mode with the `PenMode` routine. `PenPat` permits the same kind of control over the transfer pattern.

QuickDraw includes one all-purpose pen routine called `PenNormal`. This resets the pen's parameters to their default conditions. The size is one pixel by one pixel, the transfer mode is patCopy, and the pattern is black. The location is not altered by `PenNormal`, because there is no "normal" or default position.

To move the pen without performing any drawing during the relocation, use `Move` and `MoveTo`. The first is a relative move and the second moves to an absolute location in the graphics port.

Drawing lines requires the use of `Line` and `LineTo`, which are directly equivalent to `Move` and `MoveTo` except that they perform drawing as the pen moves.

Figure 5-10
A triangle with pen changes

Here is a procedure that draws a triangle in the current graphics port, changing the pen's size and pattern at each turn. Figure 5-10 shows what the display results of running this routine would be.

SetPenState(starting position)

    (assume starting position of 150,50)

LineTo(50,130)

PenPat(dkGray)

LineTo(250,160)

PenPat(ltGray)

LineTo(150,50)

PenNormal (returning pen to its original state)

Shapes

There are four basic shapes that can be drawn with single QuickDraw commands and five different things that can be done to each of these shapes. The matrix in Figure 5-11 shows the combinations of shapes and actions, with the intersections providing the QuickDraw routine name.

	Rectangles	Round-cornered rectangles	Ovals	Arcs
Frame	FrameRect	FrameRoundRect	FrameOval	FrameArc
Paint	PaintRect	PaintRoundRect	PaintOval	PaintArc
Erase	EraseRect	EraseRoundRect	EraseOval	EraseArc
Invert	InvertRect	InvertRoundRect	InvertOval	InvertArc
Fill	FillRect	FillRoundRect	FillOval	FillArc

Figure 5-11
QuickDraw shape manipulation routines

Framing a shape is the same as creating it. Painting it requires the use of either `PaintRect` (to use the port's pen patterns and thicknesses) or `FillRect` (to override the current pen data). Erasing a shape also erases any pattern with which it was filled. `InvertRect` inverts the bits encompassed by the rectangle. If all the bits are white, they turn black. If they are all black, they turn white. Action is on an individual bit basis, which permits the inversion of patterns, cursors, and other graphic items.

Rectangles: A reprise

What is not obvious from Figure 5-11 is that all the routines that frame, paint, fill, invert, or erase an oval, round-cornered rectangle, arc, or rectangle take as one argument the boundaries of the rectangle surrounding the shape. In many cases, the rectangle's boundaries are the only parameter needed by the graphic call. If your program specifies that the procedure being used should draw an oval inside a square, a circle results. But if the rectangle is not square, an oval results.

Patterns

A **pattern** is an eight-by-eight-bit image that defines a repeating design. Normally, patterns are stored as resources (see Chapter 2) and read into the system as needed by your application. A pattern's resource type is 'PAT' in the classical Macintosh world and 'PPAT' for color pixel patterns. 'PAT' must include a blank in the name to meet Macintosh's four-character requirement for resource types.

It is also possible for your program to create patterns "on the fly" using the StuffHex routine. This approach is not as efficient as creating a resource file and compiling it, but it works well where a pattern is of passing interest or use in the program. As its name implies, StuffHex "stuffs" hexadecimal values into specific areas of memory. The routine has one danger: no range-checking is performed. That makes it possible for the inattentive programmer to find his or her programs doing strange and impolite things.

Patterns are used to fill areas and as pen-drawing designs. When a pattern is used, it is automatically aligned so that it gives the appearance of a continuous stream of pattern, much like fitting wallpaper strips together so the seams are not visible.

The monochrome fill-ins light gray, gray, dark gray, and black are patterns. So are the patterns the user can select in programs like MacPaint and MacDraw.

Patterns are not actually managed by QuickDraw routines. Instead, there is a group of graphics utilities contained in the Toolbox Utilities that are separate from QuickDraw. If resources are used to store patterns, the toolbox call GetPattern loads the pattern whose resource ID is supplied. There is also a pattern list stored in the system resource file that can be accessed by indexing into it with calls to GetIndPattern.

On the new, color-capable Macintosh II, an added pattern type called **pixel patterns** is supported. Old-style monochrome bit patterns are still supported. As a programmer, you can program as if your application were going to be run only on the Macintosh II. QuickDraw has been redesigned so that if a monochrome display is being used, the patterns are converted appropriately. Pixel patterns are capable of being displayed in color, and the colors used need bear no relationship to the foreground and background colors of the graphics port in which they are displayed.

Fonts

Because all screen and printer output is handled via QuickDraw graphics routines, it will come as no surprise to you that text display is also a QuickDraw function. But text can be displayed in any of several different font families, type styles, and sizes. When QuickDraw text-creating routines are used, they in turn call appropriate Font Manager routines, which provide information to QuickDraw about the text to be displayed.

For a complete explanation of font families, type styles, and typography-related subjects, see the Font Manager chapter in Volume I of *Inside Macintosh* for the classic Macintosh. There are a few font differences for the color-capable Macintosh family members; these are described in Volume V of *Inside Macintosh*. *Technical Introduction to the Macintosh Family* also summarizes useful information about fonts.

As discussed earlier, each graphics port record has information about the font, style, size, transfer mode, and justification spacing for text drawn in that specific port. There are built-in QuickDraw routines for manipulating this information. For the most part, these routines are straightforward. `TextFont` takes as an argument an integer value representing the font to be used, `TextMode` sets the transfer mode, `TextSize` uses an integer argument to set the size in points, and `SpaceExtra` guides QuickDraw in making fully justified text look as readable as possible.

`TextFace` is the only one of these routines that requires clarification. The list of type style information is cumulative, so that if both bold and italic are specified as type style characteristics, the type will display as bold italic characters. The parameters to a `TextFace` call, then, modify the contents of the graphics port's txFace field. If your program issues a call like

`TextFace([bold,italic])`

the text will be displayed as bold and italic. You can turn an existing character trait off by using a minus sign in front of the characteristic. For example, if you have a port called thePort, its txFace field can be made to remove bold but leave everything else unchanged by a call of

`TextFace([thePort^.txFace-[bold]])`

A plus sign can be used to add a trait to a set of characteristics without knowing what those existing traits are.

QuickDraw also has a built-in procedure, `GetFontInfo`, your program can use to determine what the current graphics port's font settings are.

Once the characteristics of the text to be displayed are set by your program, displaying text is a simple matter of calling one of the three text-drawing routines: `DrawChar`, `DrawString`, or `DrawText`. Each has its place. `DrawChar` draws just one character, advances the pen to the next position, and waits for the next call. It is likely you will not often need this call because a call to either of the other routines with a single character to be printed has the same effect and is more generally usable.

`DrawString` requires that you supply as an argument a text string to be printed. `DrawText` expects you to store the information to be printed in a buffer and to supply a pointer to that buffer, a starting display position, and a length. Neither of these routines, incidentally, supplies formatting such as carriage returns or line feeds during the display of text. It is your program's responsibility to keep track of where the pen is in relation to the port's boundaries and to perform appropriate formatting.

Icons

Like fonts and patterns, icons are generally defined as resources. They are called into Macintosh memory and used by your program as needed, but they are displayed using QuickDraw routines.

An icon consists of a 32-by-32-pixel bit image stored as a block of 128 bytes in the application heap.

The management and display of icons is not a QuickDraw routine. Rather, these operations are performed by graphics utilities stored in the Toolbox Utilities as described earlier. Those utilities are `GetIcon`, which retrieves an icon from the resource file, and `PlotIcon`, which draws the icon by means of low-level calls to QuickDraw that are transparent to your program.

Cursors

Like patterns and icons, cursors are handled at least partly by Toolbox Utilities. But cursors are much more integrated into QuickDraw than either patterns or icons. Cursors are also somewhat more complex because they are active objects. Not only can the user move them around on the display as with icons, but the position of their **hot spot** when the mouse button is pressed (or even when it is not, in some applications) can cause the program to alter its course and activate procedures connected with other objects.

The QuickDraw routine InitCursor is used to start cursor activities in most applications. It sets the cursor shape to the familiar northwest-pointing arrow and also sets the **cursor level** to 0. To change the cursor on the display, your application first generally loads a cursor resource using the Toolbox Utilities GetCursor call and then makes it the currently active cursor with the QuickDraw SetCursor routine.

The cursor sometimes disappears in Macintosh applications. Most of the time, this disappearance is temporary and takes place when the user is typing into a window. To create this effect in your programs, you use ObscureCursor. This routine hides the cursor only until the next time the user moves it with the mouse or other pointing device, at which time it reappears where it was when it was obscured.

There are times, though, when you want the cursor hidden not just until it is moved but until some specific action or event occurs. In those situations, you use HideCursor and ShowCursor. Calls to these routines must be balanced; for every call to HideCursor there must be an offsetting call to ShowCursor. Failure to observe this requirement is a frequent source of programming problems on the Macintosh. HideCursor decrements the cursor level by one and ShowCursor increments it by one. Only when the cursor level is 0 is the cursor visible. This permits you to nest routines that affect whether the cursor is displayed or not and then walk the program back up through the nested calls to a point where it is appropriate to show the cursor again.

Regions

Unlike most graphics packages, which can manipulate only simple geometric shapes, QuickDraw can gather an arbitrary set of points into a structure called a **region.** It can then perform complex and rapid manipulations and calculations on such structures. Regions enable your programs to handle graphics at very high speed and to perform difficult and complex graphic operations.

Your program defines a region by first calling `NewRgn` to allocate space for it and then initializing it with `OpenRgn`. From that point until you use `CloseRgn` to indicate you are done creating this region, no drawing takes place on the screen itself unless you force it to do so. To define a region, you create a line and a shape that determine the outline of the region and its boundaries. A region should consist of one or more closed loops (see Figure 5-12).

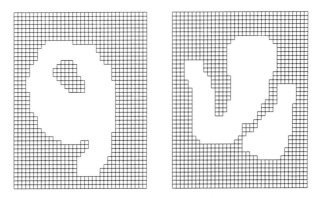

Figure 5-12
Regions

Within the memory constraint of 32K, you can create any kinds of shapes within regions that you like. When the region has been de-fined and saved, it can be called into memory from the disk and become the object of numerous manipulation and calculation calls. Regions can be copied, framed, painted, erased, inverted, and filled just like the regular geometric shapes discussed earlier. Two regions can be compared and their intersections and noncoincidental points located.

❖ *Note:* You should never use regions with any image that will be printed. The LaserWriter's firmware does not support regions.

Pictures

Another powerful idea for grouping graphic objects in QuickDraw is the **picture.** You can think of a picture as a script that records all the objects created within a graphics port and then plays them back later under program control. When you call up a graphic object saved as a picture, QuickDraw scales the drawing to a destination rectangle you supply, called the *picture frame.* This is a fast and flexible way of displaying graphic information generated by one program in another program that need not know anything about how the graphic was created.

Pictures are stored as 'PICT' resources, frequently stored in files with a type 'PICT'.

The differences between pictures and regions are not obvious at first glance:

☐ Regions have irregular boundaries, whereas pictures always fall within rectangles.

☐ Regions confine themselves to lines and shapes, whereas any kind of drawing can take place within the frame of a picture.

☐ Pictures are automatically resized when they are displayed in a rectangle that is larger or smaller than the one in which they were created, whereas regions do not change size simply by being redisplayed.

To create a new picture, use the `OpenPicture` routine. This routine both allocates the space for the new picture and causes QuickDraw to start recording drawing commands. When you are through drawing the picture, you can use `ClosePicture` to stop recording graphics commands. When the picture is saved on disk, you can simply use `DrawPicture` to display the picture after loading it into memory with the Toolbox Utilities Routine `GetPicture`.

Polygons

There is a whole class of shapes called **polygons** that can be created and manipulated in QuickDraw much like the regularly shaped rectangles, ovals, round-cornered rectangles, and arcs discussed earlier. In some ways, polygons are a cross between these shapes and pictures. They even take on the characteristics of a region for some purposes.

Only line-drawing routines `Line` and `LineTo` affect a polygon's shape. A polygon has an arbitrary shape and size (though, like a picture, is limited to 32K), made up of a series of points to be connected in sequence to recreate it.

Unlike a picture, but like the other shapes discussed, a polygon can be framed, painted, erased, inverted, or filled.

Color QuickDraw

The original QuickDraw supported color in a limited way. The version of QuickDraw for the Macintosh II provides a great deal more power and flexibility. But the degree to which the new Color QuickDraw routines produce a display that is pleasing and usable is as closely related to the type of monitor and video card used as it is to the routines themselves. This, of course, was never an issue on the classic Macintosh systems with built-in monochrome monitors.

The Color QuickDraw's graphics port data structure is more complex than that of the classic Macintosh structure. This is also true of bit image representation, which uses RGB space—a three-dimensional model in which each of the three additive primary colors (red, blue and green) can be assigned a value—rather than pixel images one bit in size.

Drawing in color graphics ports works essentially the same way as drawing in old-style monochrome or limited-color ports. `SetPort` accepts either type of port as an argument and the QuickDraw line and shape drawing routines work as expected.

There are also several new resource types associated with color graphics. These include the following, which are defined to differentiate them from their corresponding classic resources:

- □ 'crsr' (color cursor)
- □ 'ppat' (pixel pattern)
- □ 'clut' (color look-up table)
- □ 'cicn' (color icon)
- □ 'scrn' (screen)

Color cursors have a special set of routines to handle them, including `GetCCursor` for loading color cursors from resource files and `SetCCursor` for establishing the currently active color cursor. Other cursor calls work as with monochrome displays. Similar special routines exist to handle color icons and color pictures.

Text display under Color QuickDraw is somewhat different, although all the routines in the earlier Macintosh are still supported.

Chapter 6

The User Interface Toolbox

This chapter introduces the five most important and often-used parts of the User Interface Toolbox besides QuickDraw (which is covered in Chapter 5). It describes the basic functions of each part, outlines the fundamental programming approaches, and explains the use of the most important routines and calls.

These routines and calls have been chosen for much the same reason a craftsman in a skilled trade chooses tools. In any toolbox, certain tools keep landing on the top of the pile because of their frequent use. It is with these tools that the craftsman becomes so skilled that using them properly is second nature. So it is with Macintosh Toolbox routines.

Writing a complete Macintosh application can be accomplished using QuickDraw, the Memory Manager (discussed in Chapter 4), and the five tools covered in this chapter:

□ the Window Manager

□ the Menu Manager

□ the Dialog Manager

□ the Control Manager

□ TextEdit

If the application involves file I/O, then the Standard File Package (discussed in Chapter 7) is also required. Other parts of the User Interface Toolbox are often needed, but they are not requisite to writing a Macintosh application that accomplishes a useful task and complies with Apple's Human Interface Guidelines.

Similarly, within each of these tools, there are some calls that are used so often that they must become part of your programming vocabulary. Those calls are covered in this chapter. Each manager has dozens of other calls not presented here, again primarily because experience shows some calls are used far more often than others.

Most Toolbox routines work by altering or using the contents of data structures. In a sense, the entire Macintosh interface is built around these data structures. This intimate relationship between routines and data structures is a key to understanding how to program the Macintosh family.

The Window Manager

The ability to display overlapping windows is one of the most obvious and significant features of the Macintosh and its User Interface Toolbox. The **Window Manager** is responsible for creating, managing, and manipulating windows on the Macintosh desktop. One of its most important functions is to keep track of overlapping windows. Your program need not keep explicit track of what portions of which windows are overlapped and which need to be redrawn on the screen when the situation changes. The Window Manager provides built-in routines to track and handle such activities; your program merely needs to know when to call on these routines.

It is easy for your programs to use windows. A window is just another graphics port as far as your program is concerned. It can draw into a window like any other graphics port with QuickDraw routines. When your program creates a window, it simply specifies a rectangle that then becomes the portion of the port known as the portRect in which all drawing takes place.

There are six standard types of windows: document windows, document windows without grow boxes, round-cornered windows, alert or modal dialog boxes, plain boxes, and plain boxes with a partially shadowed outline. These are shown in Figure 6-1. In addition, your application program can create any kind of window it needs.

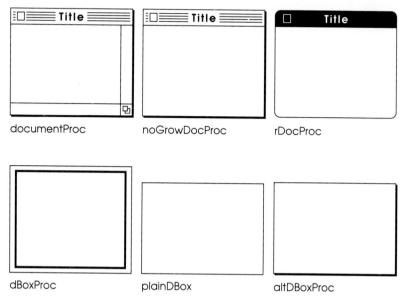

documentProc noGrowDocProc rDocProc

dBoxProc plainDBox altDBoxProc

Figure 6-1
Standard window types

Like nearly every other object your program uses, windows may be
resources. However, they need not be resources; your program
can create and dispose of windows dynamically as well.

Regions of a window

Every window, whether a standard type or one your program
creates, has a minimum of two regions. The **content region** is the
area of the window your application uses for drawing. The
structure region is the entire window (the content region plus the
window frame, which may in turn include other regions as
described below).

In addition, most windows contain one or more of the following
optional regions:

☐ the **go-away region,** which the user clicks in to close the window

☐ the **drag region,** which the user drags in to pull an outline of
   the window across the screen (making the window active if it
   isn't already)

□ the **grow region,** which the user drags in to change the size of the window while the upper left corner remains "anchored"

Figure 6-2 depicts these regions and their placement in a typical Macintosh document window.

Standard window definitions contain information about which of these regions are contained within a window.

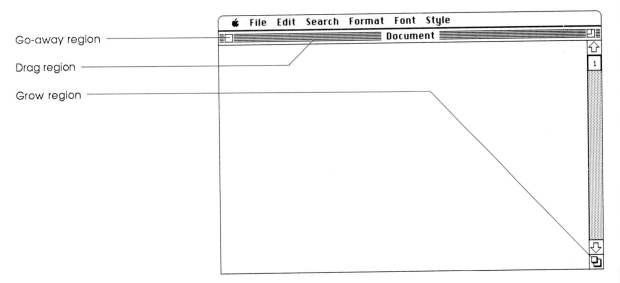

Go-away region

Drag region

Grow region

Figure 6-2
Regions of a Macintosh document window

The window record

The Window Manager stores all the information it needs about a particular window in a window record. The structure of the window record is shown in Figure 6-3. The structure is identical regardless of which member of the Macintosh family your program is running on. If your program is running on the Macintosh II, an auxiliary window record is used to retain color information needed for the window in addition to that stored in the standard window record.

This section covers only those fields of the record that are significant. A complete discussion can be found in Volume I of *Inside Macintosh*.

The first field contains the window's graphics port.

The WindowKind field identifies the window's class. A class of 2 means the window is a dialog or alert box, and a class of 8 indicates an application-defined window type. Negative numbers mean desk accessory windows. Classes 0, 1, and 3 through 7 are reserved for future use by the system.

When the visible field is True, the window is currently visible. The next two fields contain Boolean values. The first, hilited, is checked during window drawing to see if the window should be highlighted. The other, goAwayFlag, is checked to see if a close box should appear in the window when it is drawn.

The next three fields store handles to the structure region (strucRgn), content region (contRgn), and update region (updateRgn) of the window. QuickDraw uses these handles when redrawing windows. The handles are given in global coordinates.

Each window can have a title in its title bar. The field titleHandle is a handle to the title, if it has one.

Some windows contain controls such as scroll bars. If they do, the next field, controlList, contains a special handle of type ControlHandle that indicates where the list of these controls is stored. This information is used by the Control Manager, as described later in this chapter.

nextWindow is a pointer to the next window in a stack of overlapping windows—in other words, the window behind the current window. Your application should not access this data directly.

The last field of the window record, refCon, can be used by your application to store any information it wants for any purpose for which a long integer value will serve.

In color applications on the Macintosh II, an auxiliary window record is also involved, which includes a handle to the color table for the window. The structure of this record is beyond the scope of this discussion.

port
windowKind
visible
hilited
goAwayFlag
spareFlag
strucRgn
contRgn
updateRgn
windowDefProc
dataHandle
titleHandle
titleWidth
controlList
nextWindow
windowPic
refCon

Figure 6-3
The structure of a
window record

Using the Window Manager

You use the Window Manager to open and close windows under program control, update windows when changes in visible windows occur, and handle mouse-generated events including selecting a window, resizing it, moving it, or closing it at the user's direction.

Initialization

Before you initialize the Window Manager, you must first initialize QuickDraw with InitGraf, and the Font Manager with InitFonts. You can then call the InitWindows routine. InitWindows draws the desktop and an empty menu bar.

Opening and closing windows

You use either NewWindow or GetNewWindow to create windows. Each of these routines returns a pointer that you can use to refer to the window it creates. NewWindow creates windows dynamically. In this routine, you supply all the pertinent information in an argument. GetNewWindow loads a predefined window resource from the appropriate resource file, then carries out the same function as NewWindow.

Here is an example of a code segment that creates a new dialog window and allocates the storage itself, and how this window would be closed.

```
MyNewWindow = NewWindow (WinBufPtr,MyNewWinRect,"My New
Window",TRUE,DOCKind,CurrWinPtr-1,TRUE,NIL);

...

CloseWindow(MyNewWindow);
```

The NewWindow routine requires that you supply eight arguments. It returns a window pointer. The arguments you must supply are, in order, as follows:

- an optional pointer to the storage location to be used in creating the window (using Nil if you want the system to allocate the memory from the heap zone)
- the boundary rectangles for the window, in global coordinates

□ an optional window title, as a string of up to 255 characters

□ a Boolean flag that is True if you want the window to be visible and False if you do not

□ an integer representing the window definition ID

□ a parameter indicating whether you want the window to be on the bottom of the current stack (in which case the value is NIL) or on top of the stack (in which case it should be set to a value one lower than a pointer to the current top window as in the above example)

□ a Boolean flag that is True if you want a go-away region to be included in the window when it is drawn and False if you do not

□ a long integer value that is the refCon (see "The Window Record" earlier in this chapter) and that your program can use any way it wishes (normally it is Nil unless some specific purpose exists for its use in your application)

The `GetNewWindow` routine only requires three arguments. The first is the resource ID of a window template stored in a resource file. The other two are the storage pointer and an address indicating where in the stack to place the new window, which are identical to those for `NewWindow`.

When a window is no longer needed, call `CloseWindow` or `DisposeWindow`. If you specifically supply the storage location for the new window, you should use `CloseWindow`. Otherwise, if memory for the new window is allocated from the heap, call `DisposeWindow` to close it.

This example uses a prestored window resource numbered 256 to create the window and lets the system allocate the memory:

```
MyNewWindow2 := GetNewWindow (256,NIL,CurrWinPtr(-1));

...

DisposeWindow (MyNewWindow2)
```

In both of the above examples, the value CurrWinPtr(−1) as an argument indicates that the window should become the top window.

Note that in either case you can supply a Nil storage pointer and the Window Manager allocates the needed storage from the heap.

Updating windows

When the Event Manager routine GetNextEvent in your main event loop reports that an update event has occurred for your application's window, you need to set up your program to permit the Window Manager to redraw the screen. In skeleton form, this procedure requires that you do the following:

1. Save the current port with a call to GetPort.
2. Use SetPort to ensure that the window is currently active.
3. Call the Window Manager BeginUpdate routine.
4. Erase the content region of your window.
5. Draw the size box (if present) and scroll bars (if in use), either in outline form if the window is inactive or in filled-in form if it is active.
6. Redraw the content region of your window.
7. Call the Window Manager EndUpdate routine.
8. Reset the port to the originally active window with another call to SetPort.

Here is an example that depicts this processing:

```
GetPort(SavePort)

SetPort(MyWindow)

BeginUpdate(MyWindow)

DrawGrowIcon(MyWindow)

DrawControls(MyWindow)

RedrawContentRegion(MyWindow)

EndUpdate(MyWindow)

SetPort(SavePort)
```

Normally, your program redraws the entire content region of your application window. It may, however, redraw only the visible portion of the window. In either case, screen updating is automatically confined to that portion of the window that needs updating.

Of mice and windows

A mouse-down event also affects windows. Depending on where the mouse is pressed in relation to your window, you do one of the following:

- ☐ Make your window the active window with `SelectWindow`.
- ☐ Resize it with `GrowWindow` and `SizeWindow`.
- ☐ Relocate it with `DragWindow`.
- ☐ Use `TrackGoAway` and, if appropriate, call `CloseWindow` or `DisposeWindow` if the user wants the window closed.
- ☐ Call the Control Manager routine `FindControl` if the window contains controls and the mouse-down event took place in the content region.

These routines are straightforward and self-explanatory, with the exception of the `TrackGoAway` call. The go-away region is unique among the features of the window in that the user can click in it intending to close the window and then change his mind. In that event, you obviously don't want to close the window. `TrackGoAway` simply determines whether the mouse is still in the go-away region when the button is released. If it is, `TrackGoAway` returns a Boolean True and your program should close or dispose of the window, depending on how storage was originally allocated for it.

The following example uses the classic main event loop approach to determining what to do in response to a mouse-down event. This assumes that a mouse-down event has been detected in your application's window and processes the event accordingly.

```
If event is in content region
        and if window is not currently active
                SelectWindow (MyWindow)
        else if window has controls
                FindControl (Location, MyWindow, ScrollBar)
If event is in grow region
        GrowAmount=GrowWindow (MyWindow, Loc, StartSize)
        SizeWindow (MyWindow, Width, Height, TRUE)
If event is in drag region
        DragWindow (MyWindow, StartingPt, BoundaryRect)
If event is in go-away region
        CloseIt=TrackGoAway (MyWindow, goAwayPoint)
        If CloseIt returns TRUE
                CloseWindow (MyWindow)
                {OR DisposeWindow (MyWindow)}
```

The Menu Manager

Menus allow users to examine commands available to them and to select one without having to remember Command key combinations or special keys. If you've ever used a Macintosh, you are familiar with how menus work from the user's perspective.

The **Menu Manager** contains the routines and data structure that make the implementation and management of menus possible.

If you have programmed in other microcomputer environments that use a menu-driven approach to design, Macintosh menus may seem strange to you, both in how they are built and in how the user sees and uses them. In older-style programming, a menu-driven approach meant that the user was steered into the application by a series of increasingly focused menu choices. Thus there was always a master menu that gave users a set of options. Once they had selected one of them, all of the other functions of the menu screen became inaccessible unless they returned to one of them. Each new submenu narrowed the choices until a single, definable command could be discerned by the program. At that point, the program carried out the user's command and then returned to some point in the hierarchy of menus.

On the Macintosh, the user sees the menus not as successively narrower sets of alternatives but as a smorgasbord of all the choices available to him or her in the application. Macintosh users are not steered into the program. Rather, they drive the program and tell it what they want to do next.

This is all directly related, incidentally, to the idea of modeless programming that, as you saw in Chapter 1, is a key idea in Macintosh program design and implementation.

Beginning with System version 4.1, Macintosh menus take on a hierarchical capability. Under this design, menus can have submenus glued to their right sides. Figure 6-4 shows a classic Macintosh menu pulled down, and Figure 6-5 shows the same menu with a hierarchical add-on choice. This section applies to both types of menu.

Figure 6-4
A classic Macintosh menu

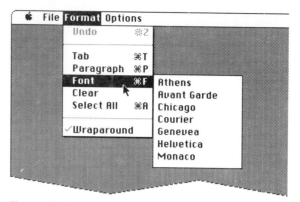

Figure 6-5
A hierarchical menu on the Macintosh II

Apple's Human Interface Guidelines strongly urge you to avoid using hierarchical menus if possible. In no case should you nest more than one hierarchical level in a menu item.

Menus as resources

Like other objects with which your Macintosh application works, menus are best handled as resources. The process for designing, storing, and retrieving resources is outlined in Chapter 2. It is important to note that menu resources must *always* be nonpurgeable.

The general appearance and behavior of a menu are determined by a routine called its **menu definition procedure,** or *menu defproc* for short. This procedure is stored in a resource file where it has a type 'MDEF'. Any action that varies from menu to menu, such as drawing it, is described in the menu definition procedure. When the Menu Manager has a function to perform with a menu, it calls the definition procedure and passes it a message that tells it which menu-dependent action to perform.

You will probably want to stay with the standard menu types, which are defined in definition procedures in the system resource file. This type of menu displays items vertically, allows each item to have an associated icon, check mark, or other symbol, permits Command-key equivalents for each item, and allows for differing the style or dimming the name of a selection that is not available at some point in the program. Color and hierarchical menu functions are also supported here. (It is possible to create other, nonstandard menu types, but the process is not described in this book.)

Using the Menu Manager

The general procedure for handling menus in a Macintosh application is constant regardless of the model of Macintosh. A color menu sometimes requires the use of calls that have slightly different names but are functionally the same as their monochrome counterparts. Hierarchical menus are handled exactly like traditional menus except in the way they are displayed. The Macintosh system knows from the setting of a particular value whether or not it is dealing with submenus and hierarchical structures.

You use the Menu Manager to set up and remove menus, respond to the user's menu selections, change menu items, and access menus and items.

Initialization

Before you initialize the Menu Manager, you must first initialize QuickDraw with `InitGraf`, fonts with `InitFonts`, and windows with `InitWindows`. `InitWindows` draws the desktop and an empty menu bar. Then you initialize menus by using the Toolbox routine `InitMenus`.

Setting up and removing menus

There are four ways your application can set up menus, depending on whether the menus are stored in a resource file and, if so, how they are stored there. All the routines for adding items to a menu bar require that you call `DrawMenuBar` after you have constructed it in memory. The calls described in this section do not affect the physical appearance of the menu bar.

If you have created a complete menu list and placed it in a resource file, GetNewMBar reads it into memory and SetMenuBar places the menu items into the menu bar. Such a **menu list** contains handles to one or more menus, along with information about the position of each menu in the menu bar. Here is an example of this process:

```
MenuHandle = GetNewMBar (13)

SetMenuBar (MenuHandle)

DrawMenuBar
```

Another, more common way of storing menus as resources is as individual menus. If you use this approach, you call GetMenu to read each menu into memory and then place them into the menu bar using InsertMenu. In this case, of course, you use a loop to read all the menus. (You must know the resource IDs of the menus to be read. This information can be obtained using the Resource Manager if necessary.) Here is an example of this approach:

```
Start loop (counter increments until all menus read)

     MenuHandle = GetMenu (counter value)

     InsertMenu (MenuHandle, 0)

     (0 means insert at end of current menu list)

End loop

DrawMenuBar
```

It is possible to create menus dynamically using NewMenu, AppendMenu to place items into each menu, and InsertMenu to place the menus and their associated items into the menu bar. This is generally not good programming practice on the Macintosh, however.

Sometimes, notably with desk accessories and fonts, it is necessary to handle menus in a way that permits your program to work regardless of how many items of a particular type are available and must be displayed. In that event, you can use AddResMenu, which looks through all open resource files for resources of a specific type and appends the names of all of them to a given menu. In this case, you use NewMenu to create each menu and InsertMenu to place each menu into the menu bar. For example, if you want to display a menu of all font choices available to the user without knowing which fonts are installed, you would use a program modeled after this example:

```
FontMenu = NewMenu (FontMenuHandle, 'Fonts')

AddResMenu (FontMenu, 'FONT')

DrawMenuBar
```

To release a menu created with `NewMenu` when it is no longer needed, call `DeleteMenu` to eliminate it from the current menu list and the menu bar. `DisposeMenu` releases the memory allocated to it. If the menu was created and loaded from a resource file, use the Resource Manager's `ReleaseResource` call instead of either of these two calls.

Responding to the user

There are two ways users can ask your program to activate a routine related to a menu choice. They can select the menu item with the mouse or use a Command-key equivalent, assuming you have provided one or the user has added one.

Apple's Human Interface Guidelines suggest that your program limit its Command-key equivalents to the most commonly used menu commands. They also discourage permitting the user to do anything with the Command-key that is not directly accessible as a menu option as well.

The only difference in the way the two types of selections are handled is at the front end of the processing. If the user selects a menu item with the mouse, it is handled through the `MenuSelect` routine. This takes care of highlighting the menu name, displaying of the menu items, tracking the mouse, and identifying the user's selection. It returns a long integer value to your program, which your application can decode to determine which menu and which menu item were selected.

❖ *Note:* Beginning with System version 4.1, you can even find out which choice the user made if the item he or she attempted to choose was dimmed at the time. This is made possible by the `MenuChoice` routine, which your program can call after `MenuSelect` returns a 0 value.

If the user selects a menu item by pressing a Command-key combination, you should call the `MenuKey` routine, passing along the character that was typed. This returns a long integer that your program processes exactly as it would a mouse selection handled by `MenuSelect`.

Typically, the part of an application responsible for handling user menu selections consists of a series of case statements based on the returned long integer value. This makes the processing of individual commands independent of the method by which the user invokes them.

Changing menu items

There are occasions when something that has changed in the environment makes it necessary to alter a menu item. For example, if the user has closed all the windows on the desktop, routines that edit or save text in those windows are no longer meaningful. Or the user might define a buffer in which to capture text being received over a telecommunications link and wish to turn the capture process on and off depending on the kind of data being transferred. In this case, your program might want to help the user keep track of whether the buffer is on or off by altering a menu item as if it were a toggle switch.

Using the Menu Manager commands GetItem and SetItem, you can exercise control over individual menu items. Using DisableItem and EnableItem, you can cause items to become unavailable and accessible again.

❖ *Note:* These two routines affect only the first 31 items in any menu. Any item whose menu ID is greater than 31 is always enabled.

You can also use InsertMenu to add a new menu to a menu bar and DeleteMenu to remove a menu from a menu bar.

In every case, once you have made a modification to a menu bar, you must still call DrawMenuBar for the user to see the effect of the change on the next menu access.

Accessing menus and items

With this powerful array of routines available to manipulate and respond to menus, the only remaining issue is how a program can identify the menu and menu item to be affected.

Each menu across the menu bar has a unique ID associated with it. If you are using resource-generated menus, you can use the menu's resource ID for its menu ID, though you are not required to do so. Some applications simply number the menus from left to right, starting with 0 for the Apple menu. Regardless of the scheme used, each menu should have a unique ID.

Within each menu, items are numbered sequentially beginning with 1 for the top, or first item, and moving down the menu. Dividing lines that are inactive as menu choices are nonetheless given numbers.

MenuSelect and MenuKey both return long integers that your program decodes to find out which menu and item were selected. The high-order word contains the menu ID and the low-order word the item number within that menu. If the user chooses the menu but then does not select an item, the high-order word is 0 and the low-order word is undefined.

If the return is 0, you can call MenuChoice to take further action. For example, if the Empty Trash option in the Finder is selected by the user when the trash is empty and the choice is dimmed, you can detect that attempt. You can then alert the user that, "The trash cannot be emptied because there's nothing in it."

Color in menus

Menus can appear in color on the Macintosh II. They can have different colors in their titles and their items can also be color-coded.

As with any other interface object, it is wise not to overdo color in menus. Use color for a purpose, not just because it is there. Again, consult *Human Interface Guidelines* for help in deciding where and how to use color in menus.

The Dialog Manager

Your application may need to interact with the user in some way other than text or graphics entry and menu selections. For example, you may want to ask the user for some information about the kind of ribbon in the printer or the baud rate to be used for a telecommunications link. Or you may want to inform the user that he or she is about to do something dangerous and offer a chance to escape gracefully from the predicament. For such purposes, you use **Dialog Manager** routines to create **dialogs** and **alerts.**

The Macintosh II permits the use of color dialogs and alerts, and programming for color is virtually the same as programming for monochrome. The few differences that do exist are beyond the scope of this book.

Types of dialogs and alerts

A modal dialog box requires the user to enter information or take some other action before processing can continue. The user's action can be as simple as pressing the Return key or clicking an OK button. Or it can be as complex as using radio buttons, check boxes, and text-editing rectangles to provide information about how the program is to proceed with the next step. The point is that a modal dialog box requires acknowledgement by the user before processing can continue.

The dialog boxes typically encountered while printing a document from a Macintosh are examples of modal dialog boxes. The user must respond to the requests before the program can continue. Modal dialog boxes do not have a close box.

Modeless dialog boxes can be thought of as providing the user with some optional help. Usually these boxes are called into action by something the user does or selects. Generally speaking, they contain close boxes because users can close them whenever they want to.

The windows called into play when a user asks a word processing program to search for text are typically modeless dialog boxes. If the user decides to cancel a search, program execution can continue where it was when the search was requested. No information is required by the program.

An alert is a special class of modal dialog predefined by the system. There are three kinds of alerts, differing only in the form of the icon they typically display in their upper left corner:

☐ A stop warns the user that a problem is about to arise.

☐ A caution alert warns of a less serious problem.

☐ A note alert provides useful or helpful data to the user in a way that requires him or her to acknowledge it.

The icons for these alerts are shown in Figure 6-6.

Stop

Note

Caution

Figure 6-6
Alert icons

Using the Dialog Manager

You use the Dialog Manager to open and close dialogs and alerts, handle the events that take place in dialogs, post alerts, and keep track of text editing in some kinds of dialogs.

Initialization

Before you initialize the Dialog Manager, you must first initialize QuickDraw with `InitGraf`, the Font Manager with `InitFonts`, the Window Manager with `InitWindows`, the Menu Manager with `InitMenus`, and TextEdit with `TEInit`. Then call `InitDialogs` to set up the dialog.

Opening and closing dialogs and alerts

Your program can either read dialogs and alerts from a resource file or create them dynamically. To get them from a resource file, use `GetNewDialog`. Creating them "on the fly" requires the `NewDialog` routine and a number of parameters describing the dialog or alert to the system.

If you allocate the storage for a new dialog explicitly, use `CloseDialog` to release its memory when you no longer need it. But if you permit the system to assign the dialog's memory, use `DisposeDialog` to release the storage.

Handling events in dialogs

The routine your program follows for reacting to events that take place in dialogs depends on the type of dialog involved.

To display and handle events in a modal dialog box, your programs call the routine ModalDialog. In itself, this routine is like a mini- application. It continuously calls GetNextEvent and examines events until it finds one it should pass to your program. The call to ModalDialog may include a filter that determines the types of events the routine should pass to the application. Normally, the system's built-in filter is adequate, but you may create your own if they're needed.

Each time an event that occurs in a modal dialog box is determined to be an event the ModalDialog should handle, the item in the dialog is returned so that the program can determine how to proceed.

Here is an example of a program segment that responds to modal dialog events:

```
Result Code = GetNewDialog (122,DialogPtr,CurWinPtr -1)

Check Result Code for error condition

If no error,

      ModalDialog (NIL,ItemHit)

      (handle event corresponding to ItemHit)
```

Handling modeless dialog boxes is a little trickier because you cannot be certain that an event that takes place when a modeless dialog box is displayed is even a dialog event. For this reason, you should call the routine IsDialogEvent. This looks at the event reported by GetNextEvent. If it is an activate or update event for a dialog window, a mouse-down event in the content region of an active dialog window, or any other type of event when the dialog window is active, IsDialogEvent returns True; otherwise, it returns False.

If the value returned by IsDialogEvent is False, you will probably want to handle the event in your main event loop as with all other kinds of events. If the return value is True, you will probably want to call the routine DialogSelect, which determines what action to take next. DialogSelect determines this based on whether the dialog item involved in the user action is enabled, whether the event creates an update or activate event for a dialog window, and whether the mouse click was inside an editable text rectangle.

Here is an example of a program segment that responds to modeless dialog events:

```
Result Code = GetNewDialog(123,DialogPtr,CurWinPtr -1)

Check Result Code for error condition

If no error,

Start loop

    GetNextEvent(NIL,theEvent)

    ...

    HandleIt = IsDialogEvent(theEvent)

    If HandleIt is True,

    DialogSelect(theEvent,DialogPtr,ItemHit)

    Handle event based on ItemHit

    otherwise, process event normally

End loop
```

Posting alerts

An alert is a special kind of modal dialog box that differs from others primarily in that it displays an icon that immediately indicates to the user of the type of alert involved. There are four calls that create alerts on the display:

□ Alert, which places no icon in the upper left corner of the box

□ StopAlert, which displays the Stop icon in the upper left corner of the box

□ NoteAlert, which displays the Note icon in the upper left corner

□ CautionAlert, which displays the Caution icon in the upper left corner

These last three calls are exactly alike except for their icons.

Text editing in dialogs

The Dialog Manager includes its own text editing commands that you can use to supplement those in TextEdit.

Normally, a dialog containing one or more editable text fields comes up with the insertion point at the left edge of the rectangle that contains the first such item. In your application, however, you may want to alter this. You may want the insertion point to appear at the end of the rectangle rather than at the beginning if you expect the user to add something to the end of the information displayed. Or you may want to start with the rectangle's text selected (highlighted) if you expect the user to either accept your suggested response or replace it entirely.

The standard editing commands are handled with calls to `DlgCut`, `DlgCopy`, `DlgPaste`, and `DlgDelete`. The text that is cut, copied, pasted, or deleted is chosen by the user. Your program uses the `SelIText` call to highlight and identify the selected text.

In every other respect, editing text in a dialog box is identical to editing text that appears anywhere under the control of TextEdit.

The Control Manager

Within dialogs and some other types of window, your program often places controls, including scroll bars, check boxes, and buttons. The **Control Manager** displays and manages these.

❖ *Note:* The Macintosh II supports color controls, but in every aspect examined here, programming controls do not vary from one system to another.

Every control "belongs" to a particular window. When displayed, the control appears within that window's content region; when manipulated with the mouse, it acts on the window. All coordinates pertaining to the control are given in the window's local coordinate system. It is essential that any window in your program containing controls have an upper left corner at coordinates (0,0) when controls are drawn. Because almost all Control Manager routines can redraw a control, it is a good idea to change the coordinate system of a window back to local before calling *any* Control Manager routine. You do this using the `GlobalToLocal` call discussed in Chapter 5.

Controls with more than one part

Most controls have only one part. A button is either on or off. A check box is either checked or not. But some controls, most notably scroll bars, have many parts, each of which has its own action. User-defined gauge-type controls are also likely to have more than one part.

Many Control Manager routines accept a part code as a parameter or return one as a result. A **part code** is an integer between 1 and 253 that identifies a particular part of a control. Each type of control has its own set of part codes, assigned by the program when defining the type or set up in advance by the system for the standard control types.

Important   Do not use part codes 254 and 255. Code 254 is reserved for future use, and 255 is used to mean the entire control is inactive.

Table 6-1 shows the part codes for the standard control types defined by Macintosh. There is no part code for a radio button because it is defined the same as a check box.

Table 6-1
Part codes for standard control types

Part	Code	Purpose
inButton	10	Simple button
inCheckBox	11	Check box or radio button*
inUpButton	20	Up arrow of a scroll bar
inDownButton	21	Down arrow of a scroll bar
inPageUp	22	"Page up" region of a scroll bar
inPageDown	23	"Page down" region of a scroll bar
inThumb	129	Thumb of a scroll bar

* inCheckBox applies to both check boxes and radio buttons.

Using the Control Manager

You use the Control Manager to create and remove individual controls, modify controls "on the fly," and respond to the user's manipulation of controls.

Initialization

Before using the Control Manager, you must first initialize QuickDraw with `InitGraf`, the Font Manager with `InitFonts`, and the Window Manager with `InitWindows`. In most cases, you also want to initialize the Dialog Manager with `InitDialogs`, though if your controls are not being used in dialogs or alerts, that step may not be necessary.

There is no routine that initializes the Control Manager.

Creating and removing controls

A control can be read in as a resource or created dynamically by your program. The routine that creates a new control is called `NewControl`, and the routine that loads a control from a resource file is called `GetNewControl`.

You can gain insight into how controls are structured and how they work by examining the `NewControl` routine. This requires nine arguments and returns to your program a handle to the newly created control. The nine arguments, in the order in which they appear, are

□ a pointer to the window that "owns" the control

□ a rectangle outlining the location of the control in the window's local coordinate system

□ the control's title, as a string of up to 255 characters

□ a Boolean flag indicating whether or not the control is visible, which results in the control being immediately drawn if True and stored for later display if False

□ an initial value setting for the control

□ a minimum value setting for the control

□ a maximum value setting for the control

□ the control definition ID for this type of control

□ a field called refCon used only by your application for whatever purpose you desire

" *The Macintosh user interface is transparent because it's supposed to be. Like anything transparent, it takes a lot of work to get it that way.* "

Harry Chesley,
independent developer

The three value settings are meaningful only for controls that retain a setting such as check boxes or radio buttons (which retain an on-off condition) and scroll bars (which retain a position setting relative to some begin and end points). For boxes and buttons, set the minimum value to 0 (off) and the maximum to 1 (on). For scroll boxes and other gauge-type controls, set the values at appropriate levels. For example, they might be used to indicate the number of lines of text or the number of filenames to be displayed.

`GetNewControl` requires only the resource ID of the control to be read and the window with which to associate it. All other information for the control is stored in the resource file.

Notice a difference between the Control Manager and the Menu Manager: there is no need to redraw the window or controls to cause them to be displayed after modifications. If you declare them to be visible, they are displayed at once.

You can remove a single control from a window with the `DisposeControl` routine. To dispose of all of a window's controls at once, use `KillControls`.

Modifying controls

A control can be made visible or invisible, moved, or resized. It is often necessary to do one or more of these in response to the user's interaction with your program.

To make a control disappear from the window, you use the `HideControl` routine. To make a specific control appear, you use `ShowControl`. To relocate a control, the Control Manager provides the `MoveControl` routine, and to resize it, the `SizeControl` routine.

For example, if the user changes the size of a document window that contains a scroll bar, your program needs to move and resize the scroll bars appropriately. You call `HideControl` to make the existing control invisible to the user, `MoveControl` and `SizeControl` to change its location and size in accordance with the new dimensions of the window, and `ShowControl` to redisplay the scroll bars as changed. (You have to do this processing twice if the window has both horizontal and vertical scroll bars.)

Here's another example. If you have a control in a dialog box set up by your program that has no meaning in certain circumstances, you might want to dim it. There is no explicit procedure for dimming a control, but the process is straightforward. Store two copies of the same control, one called ActiveWhatsit and one called InactiveWhatsit, with the latter using a dimmed characteristic. Then when you need the inactive version, just use `HideControl` to remove the incorrect one from the window, `GetNewControl` or `NewControl` to load the new one, and `ShowControl` to display it.

Responding to the user

All control activity generated by the user requires the use of the mouse. As a result, your program's main event loop focuses on this processing through its management of the mouse-down event. After receiving such an event, you use `FindWindow` to determine the part of the window in which the button was pressed and `FindControl` for that window if it was pressed in the content region.

If a control has been activated, and if it is a standard control type, call `TrackControl` to determine whether the user changes his or her mind about making the selection. If `TrackControl` returns True, meaning that the user did not relocate the mouse outside the control before releasing the button, then your application must react accordingly.

When `TrackControl` is used, it handles highlighting of the control. It also manages dragging in a scroll bar and responses to mouse clicks in other parts of the scroll bar. If, however, the mouse action is in a button, check box, or radio button, your program must process it. This includes ensuring that all inconsistent radio buttons are turned off when an application-defined button is selected.

If the control involved is one that retains a setting, you use `GetCtlValue` to find out what that setting is. This generally determines the processing to be undertaken.

TextEdit

TextEdit is designed for dealing with small amounts of text rather than with full-featured word processing.

Text rectangles that appear in dialogs are examples of places where TextEdit routines are typically used. Unformatted text processors, such as desk accessories doing text editing while engaged in telecommunications or other activities, are another example. A fully capable word processor such as MacWrite does not use TextEdit routines because such programs typically need more sophistication than is built into TextEdit.

Keep in mind that this is a discussion of editable text. If you want to display a message that the user is not expected or permitted to edit using TextEdit routines, you should use the `TextBox` routine.

Each block of editable text has associated with it an edit record and an optional style record. If the text is all set in a single font, size, and face, there is no need for a style record. An **edit record** has 31 fields, 11 of which are summarized in Figure 6-7. The other fields are used internally or are of little interest to you at this point.

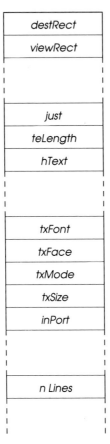

Figure 6-7
Partial contents of an edit record

Two important rectangles

Two rectangles in the edit record come into play when you use TextEdit: the destination rectangle and the view rectangle. The **destination rectangle** is the rectangle in which the text is drawn. The **view rectangle** is the rectangle in which the text is actually visible. In other words, the view of the text drawn in the destination rectangle is clipped to the view rectangle. Figure 6-8 depicts this relationship.

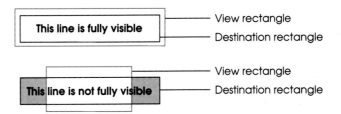

Figure 6-8
Destination and view rectangles

Your program specifies both of these rectangles, defining them by the local coordinates of the window's graphics port. It is a good idea to inset the destination rectangle at least four pixels from the left and right edges of the port's boundaries.

Edit operations may, of course, lengthen or shorten text. If the text becomes too long to fit into the destination rectangle, it is simply drawn beyond the end of the rectangle. Each line is subject to word wrapping so that if it grows too long, it automatically wraps to the left edge of the next line.

Other edit record fields

The Just field contains an integer determining whether the text is left-justified (0), centered (1), or right-justified (−1). The teLength field defines how long the text string is, and the LText field contains a handle to the text being edited.

Four fields—txFont, txFace, txMode, and txSize—describe the text in the event it is displayed in one font, face, and size. If a style record is in effect, as indicated by a −1 in the txSize field, then the txFont and txFace fields combine to become a pointer to the style record.

The inPort field identifies the graphics port in which the text is displayed. The nLines field contains an integer with the number of lines of text in the block.

The style record

The **style record** uses pointers to style tables to define "runs" of characters with a common style. A separate record is created for each run. A run is defined as any consecutive number of characters for which all style information remains the same.

Using TextEdit

You use TextEdit to open and close edit records, keep track of the user's editing operations, and handle scrap transfers.

Initialization

Before you initialize TextEdit, you must first initialize QuickDraw with `InitGraf`, the Font Manager with `InitFonts`, and the Window Manager with `InitWindows`. Then call the `TEInit` routine.

Opening and closing edit records

To allocate an edit record, call `TENew` and use the handle it returns to deal with most other TextEdit routines you encounter. When you are finished with an edit record and want to remove it, call `TEDispose`.

Tracking and managing the user's editing operations

TextEdit must respond to many kinds of events triggered by the user's activation of the keyboard or the mouse. Tracking and managing each action taken by the user in an edit record requires some planning in your programming.

When a mouse-down event occurs in the view rectangle of the window and the window is active, you call `TEClick`. If the Shift key is being held down at the same time, you pass this information to the `TEClick` routine to indicate that extended selection is in effect. The first thing `TEClick` does is unhighlight any previously highlighted text. If the mouse moves, the routine expands or shortens the selection range accordingly. A double-click selects the word under the cursor and subsequent dragging expands or shortens the selection a word at a time.

If no dragging occurs, then the mouse click repositions the I-beam cursor to indicate the insertion point.

Depending on whether there is any text currently selected or stored in the local TextEdit scrap, a key-down, auto-key, or mouse event can trigger any of several TextEdit routines.

If no text is selected and a simple key-down event is detected, the TEKey routine inserts characters and deletes those backspaced over. If text is selected, TEKey replaces it with the newly typed text, deleting the selected text with the first new keystroke passed to it.

```
TEditHandle = TENew (destRect, viewRect)

    Start loop

        TEIdle (TEditHandle)

        . . .

        (Key-down event detected in main event loop)

        TEKey (KeyPressed, TEditHandle)

        . . .

    End loop
```

With text selected, if the user selects a cut command (generally from a menu or with the Backspace key), the TECut routine removes the selection range from the text and places it in the system Scrapbook. If the user selects a cut operation with no text selected, the local scrap is emptied. A copy operation is performed similarly except that the text is not removed from the text record. TECopy is the routine that handles this task. TEDelete is a sort of flip side of TECopy: it removes the text from the edit record but does not place it into the scrap.

With or without text selected, if the user selects a paste command, the TEPaste routine inserts the contents of the local scrap into the edit record. Text already in the record is replaced by the pasted text, and the removed text is not placed in the local scrap. If no text is selected when the paste operation is performed, the pasted text is placed at the insertion point, which is then moved to the end of the pasted text.

```
TEditHandle = TENew (destRect,viewRect)

    Start loop

        TEIdle (TEditHandle)

        . . .

        (menu cut event detected in main event loop)

        TECut (TEditHandle)

        . . .

        (menu paste event detected in main event

        loop)

        TEPaste (TEditHandle)

        . . .

    End loop
```

Another way of placing new text in an existing text edit record is to use the TEInsert routine. This requires that you supply as an argument the text to be inserted.

You can use TEScroll to scroll text up, down, left, or right, using scroll bars in the text-editing window if they exist.

Chapter 7

File Management

In many ways, programming with Macintosh disk files is nearly identical to working with disk files on any other microcomputer. The file structure is hierarchical. The process of opening, reading, writing, and closing files will be familiar.

There are, however, three new ideas to understand. First, Macintosh disks and volumes can be *mounted* (available) or *unmounted* (unknown to the system). Second, files have two streams of bits associated with them instead of the usual single-stream design. These two streams are called the **resource fork** and the **data fork** and are present (though possibly empty) in all Macintosh files. Finally, the Macintosh includes a powerful and easy-to-use interface from which the user can select a filename to open or save information into. These operations are handled by the Standard File Package covered later in this chapter.

Before discussing these new ideas, this chapter presents some of the details of how files are stored and structured on the Macintosh.

Documents and applications

Macintosh files can be thought of as falling into two categories: documents and applications. It is often, but not always, possible to differentiate the two by the nature of the icon used to represent a file on the Macintosh desktop (see Figure 7-1). An **application file** contains the program code created by the programmer through a development environment. A **document file** contains the information on which the program operates. Most applications by nature can have multiple documents with which they work.

Application   Document

Figure 7-1
Application and document
file icons

This chapter discusses only document files. In fact, it is concerned only with the data fork of a document file, though the term *file* will be used to refer to the data fork. Application file structure, storage, and access are controlled by the development system in which you do your programming.

Unlike most traditional microcomputer files, a document file can be selected by the user in such a way that it automatically executes the program for which it is designed. The process by which you set up a document file type to work with your applications is called **bundling.**

An outline of file interaction

Figure 7-2 depicts the typical file interaction that takes place between your program and the user when the time comes to access a file on the disk. For example, if your program is a data base application and the user wants to open a data file with names, addresses, and other important customer information, the user chooses the Open option from the standard File menu. At that point, your program calls the Standard File Package into play.

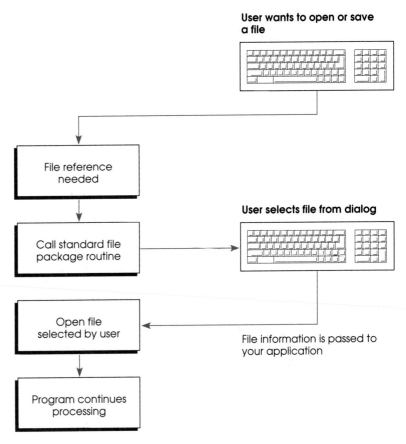

Figure 7-2
Basic file interaction

The Standard File Package puts up a dialog box in which the user can select the drive, volume, folder, and document to be loaded into the program. Your program can determine what types of files the user will be permitted to select from in this dialog.

When the user selects a file from the Standard File Package's dialog, the File Manager automatically passes to your program the infor-mation it needs to access this file. You do not need to keep track of where on which disk the file is located: that job falls to the user and the Standard File Package. With this information available, your program simply accesses the file designated by the user.

The information returned by the Standard File Package to your program is a file identifier composed of the filename plus the **volume reference number.** This is a unique number identifying the volume and, if needed, the directory to be used. It is in effect for the entire time an application is running. This number is automatically assigned by the system when the volume is mounted. The combination of this unambiguous volume reference number and the name of the file makes it possible to address files with the same names that reside in different subdirectories of different volumes, even if the volumes have identical names.

Types and creators

Each Macintosh data file has two other attributes that are important: a type and a creator. Both of these are assigned by your program when the user creates a file with your application.

File types

A **file type** is defined as a four-character string that describes, in somewhat cryptic form, the kind of information the file contains. For example, a file containing text without special formatting (fonts, styles, and so on) is almost always a file of type 'TEXT'. MacPaint files have the type 'PNTG' (created from the word "PaiNTinG").

To ensure uniqueness of file type designators, Apple maintains a registry of four-character descriptors. Register your four-character type code with Apple before finalizing it.

By convention, application program files have a type of 'APPL'.

Creators

In addition to the file type, each file has a **creator** associated with it. This creator code determines which application should be launched when this file is opened from the Finder.

Like the file type, the creator must be unique. Apple maintains a registry of four-character creator codes, and you must register yours before finalizing it.

File manipulation and the Standard File Package

One aspect of Macintosh programming that quickly became standardized was the implementation of a File menu from which the user could choose files to be opened and saved. The Standard File Package's SFGetFile and SFPutFile routines provide an efficient and effective way for your program to open and save files. These routines are called by your program when the user chooses a file from the File menu with Open, Save, Save As, or New.

SFGetFile in operation

The SFGetFile routine displays a dialog box listing the names of a specific group of files from which the user can select one to be opened. It then repeatedly gets and handles events until the user either chooses a filename or aborts the command by clicking Cancel in the dialog box. It reports the results of this by filling fields in a **reply record.**

This routine takes seven system-supplied parameters. The most important are

☐ the coordinates of the upper left corner of the dialog box to be displayed

☐ a pointer to a procedure that filters the types of files to be shown to the user

☐ an integer that tells the system how many types of files are to be shown to the user

□ a list of file types to be shown to the user

□ a pointer to a reply record in which the routine stores the results of its interaction with the user so that your application can monitor what took place and determine its next steps accordingly

There are two ways your program can ensure that when the user is shown a dialog box by the Standard File Package, only files appropriate to your application are displayed. First, it can simply pass an array of file types to the Standard File Package, which will automatically handle the filtering process. If this is not sufficient, it can supply a procedure that looks at each file in the directory on a file-by-file basis to determine whether to show them to the user or not. This approach might be useful, for example, if you want only to show the user files created after a certain date or containing certain kinds of information.

The File Open dialog box

Figure 7-3 shows a standard File Open dialog box generated by the Standard File Package. It shows all of the folders and individual documents that are not in folders. The user can open a document by the usual means of double-clicking its name or by selecting its name and clicking the Open button.

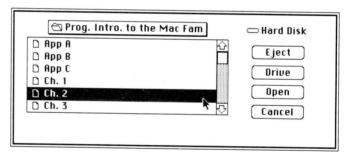

Figure 7-3
A File Open dialog box

On hierarchical file systems, this dialog is designed to permit the user to move around in the hierarchy of files by clicking in the rectangle above the file list. This rectangle contains the name of the current volume and folder whose contents are being shown. When the user clicks there (see Figure 7-4), a pop-up menu appears showing the complete hierarchy above this volume and folder combination. The user can then move directly to any of those levels by selecting it exactly as he selects items from any other menu. The Standard File Package handles all of this hierarchical movement for you.

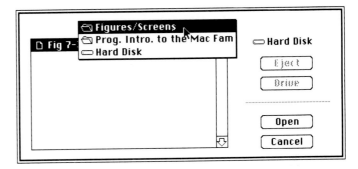

Figure 7-4
A hierarchy list in a File Open dialog box

The reply record structure

A reply record used by the Standard File Package routines contains six fields. The most important of these are

☐ a Boolean flag that is True if the user made or affirmed the Save or Open selection, and False if Cancel was clicked, in which case file operations should not be performed

☐ the reference number of the volume directory accessed

☐ the name of the file

SFPutFile in operation

The SFPutFile routine displays a dialog box (see Figure 7-5) requesting that the user specify a file to which data will be written. It then repeatedly gets and handles events until the user either confirms the command after typing a filename or aborts the command by clicking Cancel in the dialog box. It reports the results of this interaction to your application by filling fields in a reply record exactly as SFGetFile does.

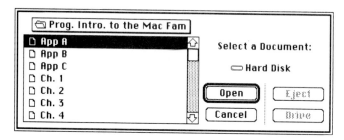

Figure 7-5
A typical SFPutFile dialog box

A File Save dialog box is nearly identical to the File Open dialog box, except that the names of individual documents are dimmed. The user can open any folder and thereby cause the current file to be saved in that folder.

SFPutFile also detects duplicate filenames and asks the user to confirm the overwriting of an existing file by the new one. It can also detect a locked disk, a condition that cannot be overridden in software. In either case, it displays an appropriate dialog box.

Program file use and the File Manager

The File Manager is part of the Macintosh Operating System. It permits your programs to deal with information stored on the disk without concerning itself with the fine points of the disk driver or physical locations of information. Your program can read and write blocks of data of any size in a single file operation. The File Manager takes care of converting your high-level requests into operations that carry out the disk functions.

The Macintosh uses a mark approach to file management. Each byte in the file is uniquely addressable by its distance from the start of the string of bytes that constitute the file. By convention, the first byte is 0, the second byte is 1, and so forth.

Each open file has a **mark,** or position indicator, associated with it by the File Manager. When a file is first opened or created, its mark is set to byte 0. Each time a read or write operation occurs, the mark is moved accordingly. Attempting to read past the logical end-of-file (EOF) creates an error condition with which your program must deal.

Return codes from disk I/O operations

All high-level File Manager routines return an integer that can be translated into an operating-system error code, called an OSErr. It is important to the successful operation of your program that you check this error code after each I/O operation invoked by your program.

A result code of 0 (referred to in Macintosh parlance as noErr) means that the operation was successfully completed and your program can continue processing. Other common result codes return to your program as negative integers in the range of −33 to −127, as shown in Table 7-1.

Table 7-1
Some I/O result codes of type OSErr

Error Number	Name	Meaning
0	NoErr	Successful completion
−33	DirFulErr	Directory full
−34	DskFulErr	Disk full
−36	IOErr	General disk I/O error
−38	FNOpnErr	File not open
−39	EOFErr	Attempt to read past end of file
−40	PosErr	Attempt to position before start of file
−41	MFulErr	System heap full
−42	TMFOErr	Attempt to open too many files
−43	FNFErr	File not found
−44	WPrErr	Disk is write-protected
−45	FLckdErr	File locked
−46	VLckdErr	Volume locked
−192	ResNotFound	Resource not found
−194	AddResFailed	Attempt to add resource failed
−196	RmvResFailed	Attempt to remove resource failed

Accessing file data

Using File Manager routines, your program can create, open, read, write, and close disk files. Each of these operations is carried out by a function that returns an I/O result that your program should check. The general form for a disk I/O operation is

```
Result Code = DiskOperation(Parameters)
```

Creating new files

The `FSCreate` routine creates a new file. It requires four para-meters: the name of the file, the reference number identifying the volume and directory to be used, the file creator, and the file type. (These last two fields are used by the Finder in locating and working with files.) Generally, the creator is a code used by your application. If you have a program that performed statistical opera-tions, for example, you might arbitrarily give files it creates the creator label 'STAT'. (If you do create such file types, it is a good idea to register them with Apple Developer Services. This ensures that no two applications use the same file type designators.)

Here is a sample of an `FSCreate` call:

```
Result Code = FSCreate ("TestFile", VRefNum, 'STAT', 'TEXT')
```

Opening existing files

The `FSOpen` routine opens an existing file. The routine requires three parameters: the filename, a volume reference number, and a variable in which the function can return an integer value representing the file's path reference number. This last parameter is used by other routines to access the file once it is opened.

Here is a sample of an `FSOpen` call:

```
Result Code = FSOpen ("TestFile", VRefNum, PathRef)
```

Reading data from open files

Data stored in existing files that have already been opened is accessed with the `FSRead` routine. Your program calls `FSRead` with the file reference number (the path reference number returned by `FSOpen`), the number of bytes to be read, and a pointer to the buffer in which the data is to be stored. Reading begins wherever the current file position pointer is located, so if your intent is to read from the beginning of the file, you may have to call `SetFPos` before you begin reading.

If the number of bytes you ask to read takes you past the file's EOF marker, `FSRead` leaves the marker at the end of the file and returns an error (eofErr). In any case, the number of bytes actually read is contained in the same field used to tell `FSRead` how many bytes to read.

Here is a sample of an `FSRead` call:

```
Result Code = FSRead (VRefNum, ByteCount, BufferPtr)
```

where ByteCount is a variable that has been set to the number of bytes to be read and BufferPtr is pointing to a large enough buffer in memory to store the data retrieved.

Reading and writing operations are affected by where the file position marker is located and where the EOF is found. You can find out where the current file position marker is by calling `GetFPos`, and you can change it with `SetFPos`. Similarly, you can find and change the EOF marker's position with `GetEOF` and `SetEOF`.

Writing information to disk files

Data is stored on disk files with the `FSWrite` routine. It has the same arguments as `FSOpen`. `FSWrite` operates on data beginning at the buffer pointer location and continuing for the number of bytes requested to be written. It attempts to write them to the open file whose access path is specified in the call.

After the write is completed, the number of bytes actually written is returned in the same variable used to store the number of bytes requested to be written when the routine was called.

Here is a sample of an `FSWrite` call:

```
Result Code = FSWrite (VRefNum, ByteCount, BufferPtr)
```

Closing files

Your program closes an open file with a call to the routine `FSClose` and the file's path reference number as its sole argument. You should know, however, that there is no guarantee that any bytes have been written to the disk before it is closed unless your program first calls `FlushVol` (see "An Example of File Handling").

Managing volumes

FlushVol is one of the more important File Manager routines. Data stored in a volume's buffer, along with descriptive information about the volume (such as date created, date last modified, and remaining storage capacity), is only written to the disk when this routine is executed. It is important to any file-handling routine, therefore, that you include FlushVol at strategic points in your program. Most experienced Macintosh programmers use FlushVol after any FSClose call.

An example of file handling

Here is a small example of a program fragment that would handle opening a file, processing editing actions, and writing the record back on the disk. It is, of course, necessarily brief and somewhat incomplete (it does not, for example, spell out the editing processing in detail), but it provides a skeleton for you to develop your own code for similar tasks.

```
File Open menu event detected in main event loop
SFGetFile (StdLoc,"Get which file?",NIL,1,
       theTypeList,NIL,Result Code)
Check Result Code for error condition
If no error,
       Result Code = FSOpen (fileName,VRefNum,
              FileRefNum)
       Check Result Code for error condition
       If no error, continue processing user editing
       ...
File Save or Save As menu event detected in
       main event loop
SFPutFile (StdLoc,"Save file under what name?",
       ' ', NIL, Result Code)
Check Result Code for error condition
If no error,
       Result Code = FSClose (FileRefNum)
       Check Result Code for error condition
       If no error,
       FlushVol (NIL,VRefNum)
```

Chapter 8

Development Tools

This chapter moves beyond the specific programming techniques, calls, and commands needed to develop Macintosh applications and focuses on the development tools available. It begins by providing an overview of Apple's Macintosh Programmer's Workshop (MPW). More and more development work is being done within MPW both because of the environment it provides and because of Apple's support of it.

This chapter then looks at MacApp, Object Pascal, HyperCard™, and other programming languages and environments available for the Macintosh. Finally, it discusses some debugging techniques.

The Macintosh Programmer's Workshop (MPW)

In late 1986, Apple introduced the **Macintosh Programmer's Workshop (MPW)** through the Apple Programmer's and Developer's Association (APDA). (Appendix C contains information about APDA).

MPW is a set of professional software development tools for the Macintosh consisting of the following:

☐ an editing and programming environment called the MPW Shell

☐ assemblers for the 68000 and 68020 processors

☐ a linker

☐ a resource editor

☐ a resource compiler/decompiler

☐ a debugger

In addition, separate MPW modules can be obtained to implement high-level languages within the MPW environment. These include

☐ MPW Pascal, including a set of object-oriented programming extensions

□ MPW C, along with a complete set of interfaces and libraries

□ MacApp, a fully functional program template in the form of an expandable "generic application" using object-oriented programming techniques

MPW provides numerous advantages over previous development systems for the Macintosh. These are among the more noticeable of them:

□ *Integration:* The various components of the MPW system all run within the MPW Shell environment.

□ *Command scripting:* In addition to menu commands, MPW provides a full command language. You can combine any series of MPW commands into a **command file,** or *script,* for accurate results with little or no reprogramming.

□ *Regular expression processing:* The editor in the MPW Shell allows you to search and replace using regular expressions, forming a language for describing complex text patterns.

□ *Extensibility:* You can create your own integrated tools to run within the Shell environment and can add your own menu commands to the Shell.

Figure 8-1 shows the stages of program development under MPW. Notice that MPW provides complete editing, compiling, and linking tools for resources as well as code segments.

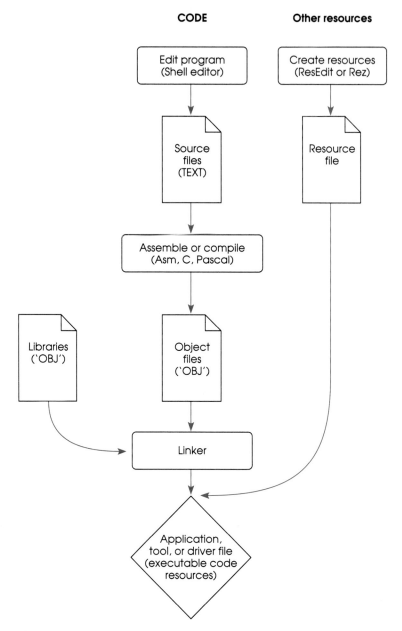

CODE   **Other resources**

Edit program
(Shell editor)

Create resources
(ResEdit or Rez)

Source
files
(TEXT)

Resource
file

Assemble or compile
(Asm, C, Pascal)

Libraries
(`OBJ`)

Object
files
(`OBJ`)

Linker

Application,
tool, or driver file
(executable code
resources)

Figure 8-1
Program development under MPW

The MPW Shell

The **MPW Shell** is an application that provides an integrated, window-based environment for program editing, file manipulation, compiling, linking, and program execution. All the other parts of MPW operate in the Shell environment. These tools can perform input and output to files and to Shell windows.

The Shell combines a command language and a text editor. You may enter commands in any window, or execute them through menus and dialogs. The command language provides text editing and program execution, including routines for passing parameters to tools, command file scripting, and I/O redirection.

The MPW Shell integrates the following components:

☐ an editor for creating and modifying text files

☐ a command interpreter for interpreting and executing commands entered in a window or read in from a file

☐ a set of built-in commands for handling files without returning to the Finder, processing variables, managing program control flow, and other tasks

Other parts of MPW

In addition to the Shell and the tools, MPW includes a debugger, a number of sample application files, and ResEdit. It also offers optional Pascal, C, and Assembler implementations.

The debugger

The MacsBug 68000 debugger is provided with MPW. MacsBug resides in RAM and allows you to examine memory, trace through a program, or set up break conditions.

Sample application source files

Source files are provided for the sample application from Volume I of *Inside Macintosh* as well as for several other sample applications. Examples are furnished in MPW Assembler, Pascal, and C and include instruction files and **makefiles** for building the sample files into applications.

ResEdit

ResEdit is an interactive, graphically based resource editor for creating, editing, copying, and pasting resources. MPW Pascal includes a set of extended Resource Manager routines that make it possible to write your own add-on resource editors for ResEdit.

ResEdit is supplied in addition to two programs called Rez and DeRez, which compile and decompile textual descriptions of resources.

MPW Pascal

In the early days of Macintosh, developers were required to use Apple's Lisa systems as development environments until Macintosh-based tools became available. For many reasons, Lisa Pascal became the standard development language for the Macintosh.

MPW Pascal is based on version 3.1 of Lisa Pascal. Lisa Pascal, in turn, was a very nearly standard Pascal, so that MPW Pascal approaches compliance with the American National Standards Institute's definition of Pascal known as ANS Pascal.

One difference between MPW Pascal and most other versions of the language is that MPW Pascal is extended to include support for object-oriented programming. (This subject is covered later in this chapter.) These object-oriented extensions, collectively referred to as Object Pascal, are extensions of Lisa's Clascal environment.

MPW C

MPW C is a complete implementation of the C programming language. It consists of the C Compiler, the Standard C Library, the Macintosh Interface Libraries, the C SANE (Standard Apple Numeric Environment) Library, and example programs.

This version of C is based on the de facto industry standard known as the Portable C Compiler (PCC) and more specifically the Berkeley 4.2 BSD VAX implementation of PCC.

MPW adds extensions to this standard C to allow calls to and from Pascal programs and Macintosh interface libraries as well as support for SANE.

The Standard C Library is a collection of basic routines that let you read and write files, examine and manipulate strings, perform data conversion, acquire and release memory, and perform mathematical operations. This library contains functions that support MPW tools.

Interfaces between C and the Macintosh ROM and RAM routines are supplied in the Macintosh Interface Libraries. Through this library, your C programs can access the routines described in *Inside Macintosh* and in this book.

The C SANE Library provides mathematical functions and supports floating-point arithmetic.

MPW Assembler

MPW Assembler reads source text and creates a file of linkable 68000 object code. It includes a number of features to help you build powerful assembly-language programs. Some of these features that are important for this discussion are

☐ broad 68000-family support—including all instructions and addressing modes for the 68000, 68010, 68020, and 68030 microprocessors, the 68851 Paged Memory Management Unit (PMMU), and the 68881 floating-point coprocessor, in all combinations

☐ powerful macro capabilities

☐ global and local variable use within macros to facilitate communication between macros

☐ full control over generation of code and data modules, and a choice of creating single object modules or a series of separate ones

☐ ability to generate Pascal-formatted and C-formatted strings

MacApp and object-oriented programming

MacApp was written at Apple to simplify the process of creating Macintosh application programs. It is essentially a complete, functional Macintosh application. You are free to take it apart, use the pieces you need, add portions of code to handle application-specific processing, and generally use it any way you like.

❖ *Note:* If you use MacApp to develop commercial products, you need to sign a special license to distribute run-time portions of MPW and MacApp code. This is an area where Apple Developer Services can be helpful (see Chapter 9).

Before you can understand how MacApp works and how it simplifies the programming process, you need to know something about object-oriented programming. A complete discussion of the subject is beyond the scope of this book. See Kurt Schmucker's book, *Object-Oriented Programming for the Macintosh* (Hayden, 1986), for a more in-depth presentation on the subject.

An introduction to object-oriented programming

Object-oriented programming is essentially a style of programming that uses some new constructs and concepts to change the way programs are written.

Most programs are **procedure-oriented.** They are organized around procedures and functions. In a procedure-oriented program, you decide what tasks need to be performed, and then you write procedures and functions to carry out the tasks. The data on which the procedures and functions operate is stored in variables of different kinds, including structured variables such as arrays and records.

MacApp programs are object-oriented. An object-oriented program is organized around **objects.** Objects are places for data storage, much like Pascal records, but they also have **methods,** which are routines that operate on the object's data. The essential point is that you decide on your data structures first, and then decide what routines you need to operate on the data structures. You can do that in any language; in an object-oriented language, however, you can group the data structures and the routines together into objects.

If procedures and functions are verbs and pieces of data are nouns, a procedure-oriented program is organized around verbs and an object-oriented program is organized around nouns. Imagine that you had a program that operated on dogs, mice, and cats. Further, imagine that the program needed to implement eating and running methods for the dogs, mice, and cats.

To write this in a verb-oriented (procedure-oriented) way, you could write

```
dog = RECORD
mouse = RECORD
cat = RECORD

PROCEDURE Eat(animal)
     IF animal = dog THEN eat this way
     IF animal = mouse THEN eat another way
     IF animal = cat THEN eat a third way
END

PROCEDURE Run(animal)
     IF animal = dog THEN run this way
     IF animal = mouse THEN run another way
     IF animal = cat THEN run a third way
END
```

To write this program in a noun-oriented (object-oriented) way, you could write

```
dog = OBJECT
     PROCEDURE Eat
     PROCEDURE Run
END

mouse = OBJECT
     PROCEDURE Eat
     PROCEDURE Run
END

cat = OBJECT
     PROCEDURE Eat
     PROCEDURE Run
END
```

This small example is not intended to demonstrate any advantages of object-oriented programming, but merely to illustrate the organizational difference.

What are objects?

An object is like a "machine" that does its task independently. Here are object-type declarations for some arbitrary object types called TOval and TBox. (By convention, all object-type identifiers in MacApp begin with a *T*.) Notice that although the syntax is a bit different, the declarations are organized like programs.

```
TOval=OBJECT
     boundsRect: Rect; {bounding box}
     pat: Pattern;
     PROCEDURE TOval.IOval(left,top,right,bottom: integer);
{Initialize oval}
     PROCEDURE TOval.Draw;
END;

TBox = OBJECT
     boundsRect: Rect; {bounding box}
     pat: Pattern;
     PROCEDURE TBox.IBox(left,top,right,bottom: integer);
{Initialize box}
     PROCEDURE TBox.Draw;
END;
```

The **fields** of these objects, boundsRect and pat, are declared like the fields of records. In fact, you refer to the fields of an object in the same way you refer to the fields of a record. For example, if you declare a variable of type TOval:

```
anOval: TOval
```

you can refer to the fields of the object like this:

```
anOval.boundsRect
anOval.pat
```

As you can see from the declarations of TOval and TBox, when you define an object type, you just define the interface to the procedures and functions of the object. These "private" procedures and functions are the methods of the object. You define the implementation of the methods later. This is equivalent to a FORWARD declaration in classical Pascal, in that you can have forward references within the blocks of the routines. The implementation of these routines would look much like they would outside the object-oriented world. Here is an example:

```
PROCEDURE TBox.Draw;
BEGIN
     FillRect(boundsRect,pattern);
END;
```

Just as you can refer to the global variables boundsRect and pat anywhere in the program Box, you can refer to the fields boundsRect and pat anywhere "within" an object of type TBox without qualifying those fields.

To invoke a method of an object, you refer to it in the same way you refer to a field. When you are "outside" the object anOval (in the main program or in a method of another object), you write

```
anOval.Draw
```

However, if you want to call TOval.Draw from within a method of the same object type, you just use the identifier Draw. You might write another method for TOval as follows:

```
PROCEDURE TOval.Flash;
BEGIN
    pat := white;
    Draw;
    pat := black;
    Draw;
END;
```

Each call to Draw always calls TOval.Draw. In a sense, every field and method of an object type is within the scope of the object type.

An object-type declaration is a template that defines the characteristics and capabilities (fields and methods) of objects of that type. Fields and methods are very much alike, except that each object can have different values in its fields, but every object of a given type has the same methods. To go back to the dogs, mice, and cats example, each cat may differ from other cats in weight or color, but every cat eats and runs in the same way. The methods determine the characteristics of the species; the fields determine the characteristics of the individual within the limits of the species.

Objects and inheritance

Just as species can have ancestor species from which they inherit characteristics, object types can have ancestor object types from which they inherit characteristics. As with species, the descendant type can change characteristics inherited from its ancestor. Among animals, dogs and bears are descended from a common ancestor. They both acquired the ability to walk on four legs; one or both of them changed the way that ability is implemented. Similarly, descendant object types inherit capabilities, and they may reimplement some of them.

Object Pascal

Object Pascal programs are structured around object types. Just as any variable is defined by its type, an object is defined by its object type. Unlike other kinds of types, the object type defines both the type of data structure the object has and the methods the object can perform.

Object types belong to an object hierarchy. This hierarchy makes it possible for object types to share characteristics belonging to object types above them in the object-type hierarchy. Figure 8-2 illustrates the basic Object Pascal hierarchy and introduces some fundamental Object Pascal terms.

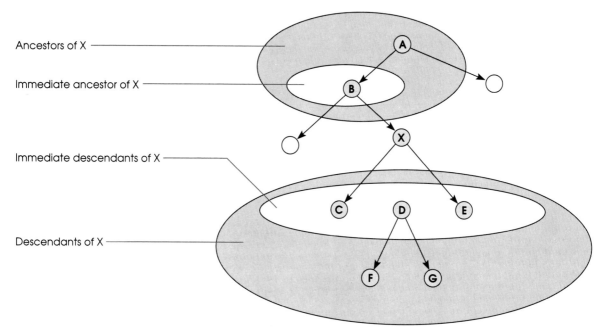

Figure 8-2
Object-type hierarchy

Every circle in Figure 8-2 is an object type. Within the hierarchy, object types have relationships. **Ancestors** are object types that are above another object type in the hierarchy—A and B are X's ancestors. **Descendants** are object types that are below another object type in the hierarchy—C, D, E, F, and G are descendents of X. An immediate descendant is an object type that is one level below another in the hierarchy—C, D, and E are immediate descendants of X. The process of declaring an immediate descendant is called **customizing** the ancestor object type. An immediate ancestor is an object type that is one level above an object type in the hierarchy—B is X's immediate ancestor.

❖ *Note:* Other texts use a different set of terminology in describing Object Pascal, derived from the terminology used for Smalltalk. A *class* is equivalent to an object type. A *subclass* is equivalent to an immediate descendant. *Subclassing* is equivalent to customizing. A *superclass* is equivalent to an immediate ancestor. And a *message* is equivalent to a method call.

One object type, TObject, is necessary for writing Object Pascal programs. TObject defines the most general characteristics of all Object Pascal objects. For example, TObject provides a general method for copying an object and a method for discarding an object. Additional object types in a program are defined by the programmer.

Object Pascal and MacApp

Object Pascal was developed in conjunction with MacApp, the expandable Macintosh application. MacApp is made up of libraries of Object Pascal code with predefined object types that provide certain standard functions for applications, essentially implementing the Macintosh user interface. MacApp thus provides standard Macintosh application behavior. When you write a MacApp program, you add extensions to MacApp by creating object types and methods to perform the work of your application.

One of the most important features of Object Pascal is that method calls are used to tell an object to perform a method on itself. This means that MacApp can tell one of the objects in your code to invoke a method. Typically, MacApp calls a method in response to a user action such as choosing a command from a menu. In a case like that, your object type is a descendant of one of the MacApp types, the MacApp object type defines methods that you override, and your implementation of the called method is invoked.

An introduction to MacApp

MacApp was written to take care of most of the standard behavior of a Macintosh program. Because it is written in an object-oriented fashion, you can write your application as an extension of MacApp, essentially particularizing the generalized objects provided by MacApp.

MacApp declares six major object types, with each basic object type corresponding to a conceptual entity in object-oriented programming style. The six entities are

□ view

□ frame

□ window

□ document

□ application

□ command

When you start a MacApp application, your main program creates and initializes the application object, and then calls the run method for that object. As a rule, the run method generates a command to open an old document or to create a new one. The document object then creates the view, frame, and window objects accordingly.

The view object is unique to MacApp. You can think of it as being the surface on which an interpretation of the document's data is displayed.

The frame object is made up of the scroll bars and the content region of the document's window. The window object includes the title bar, the close box, the size box, and the zoom box.

Command objects are created by other objects to handle specific commands. Typically, one of the other five types of objects generates a command object to change itself.

Programming in MacApp

Although MacApp is presently available only in MPW Pascal with its object extensions, at this writing several third-party vendors and Apple are working on implementations of MacApp in other languages, including C and Smalltalk.

Programming a Macintosh application in MacApp is different from programming a procedure-oriented approach only in the same ways that object-oriented programming differs from traditional programming. In the case of the MPW Pascal implementation of MacApp, all the tools of the MPW environment and the MPW Shell are available to you as you develop applications in MacApp.

HyperCard as a development environment

In the summer of 1987, Apple introduced HyperCard. This product has significance for Macintosh developers for two reasons:

☐ It is available free or virtually free to all Macintosh owners, thus providing a common development environment for Macintosh applications.

☐ It includes a programming language called HyperTalk™ that, while not a full-blown language with complete access to the Toolbox, is nonetheless powerful and flexible.

A common delivery vehicle

When the Macintosh was introduced, one of the long-standing microcomputer traditions it broke was that of supplying a built-in programming language. Most microcomputers before the Macintosh included a form of BASIC either in ROM or on disk as part of the system.

There were some clear advantages to this approach. A computer that did not include or seem to the casual user to need a programming language was more inviting. In keeping with Apple's theme for the Macintosh as the computer "for the rest of us," this approach was effective.

It did, however, have one drawback. Developers could only design Macintosh applications as stand-alone, executable files if they wanted to be sure that any Macintosh owner who wished to could run their products. There was no "common language" in which every Macintosh could run other than its native machine tongue.

HyperCard is now bundled with every Macintosh sold. When it was introduced, those persons who already owned Macintosh systems could buy HyperCard for a nominal sum. Thus, there is now a language in which you can write an application without having to compile it and produce an executable file. All Macintosh owners can and should own HyperCard.

HyperTalk

HyperTalk is the language built into HyperCard. It enables even inexperienced programmers to design applications, called *scripts,* which can be executed when the user takes certain actions in the HyperCard environment. When a button is pressed, a stack is opened, a card is accessed, or information is placed into a field, an associated script written in HyperTalk can be called into action.

HyperTalk contains many object-oriented programming ideas, though it is not itself an object-oriented programming *language.* HyperTalk involves objects passing messages to other objects for execution. It includes scripts, which closely resemble methods and are tied directly to the objects that execute them.

There are five kinds of objects in HyperTalk:

☐ buttons
☐ fields
☐ cards
☐ backgrounds
☐ stacks

The basic unit of information is the card. Each card is associated with a background, and a background may be (and usually is) shared by more than one card.

The card overlays the background, and both are the size of the classic Macintosh screen. Buttons and fields can belong either to individual cards or to backgrounds. In the latter case, they appear on and are accessible from every card with that background.

Although HyperTalk was designed to be easy enough for nonprogrammers to use, professional developers find it presents a particularly comfortable and uncluttered environment in which to develop applications for which the language is sufficient.

Other programming languages and environments

Apple Computer encourages program developers to use MPW, MacApp, and HyperTalk to the extent that makes sense. Their use should result in programs that comply with the Human Interface Guidelines and are relatively easier to code and maintain. However, Apple recognizes that many other companies have devised development environments and programming languages for the Macintosh.

A complete list of the current programming languages and tools available for the Macintosh can be obtained on request from Apple's Developer Services.

Debugging Macintosh applications

Like programming, debugging is an art. And like any art, success is at least partly dependent on the right tools. In Macintosh application programming, that means one of several programs including MacsBug, TMON, or the Seawell Inspector. Each of these debuggers has its advantages and limitations. Many programmers have more than one available and use the one they think is most likely to give them the answer to the problem they are facing at the moment.

When a Macintosh program exhibits bugs of the softer variety—often called *logic errors*—there is no shortcut to debugging them. You just have to do as you do with any other system and language: step through the program and play computer until you find the error.

But a "hard crash" on the Macintosh can be debugged with a powerful debugger and some basic direction. A detailed discussion of debugging is well beyond the scope of this book. But there is an important principle to keep in mind.

Important	Any crash that occurs on a Macintosh is caused by the execution of a single MC68xxx assembly-language instruction. This alone may help take some of the mystery out of debugging.

Beyond that, there is an additional set of hints. This is from Scott Knaster, author of *How to Write Macintosh Software* (Hayden, 1986), a book that contains an extensive amount of information about debugging Macintosh programs. He suggests that there are four basic questions the programmer must ask during the debugging cycle:

☐ Where did the program crash? In other words, what was the last instruction *in your program* that was properly executed?

☐ What specifically caused the crash? Was a bad parameter passed to a Toolbox routine? Did the system run out of memory?

☐ What assembly-language instruction was the last one executed before the crash? Using breakpoints and other debugging aids in your debugging tool, you can hone in on the single assembly-language instruction that caused the problem.

☐ What caused the offending instruction to be executed? Now that you know which assembly-language instruction caused the problem, you must identify the call (usually in ROM) that caused the call to this instruction.

The best advice is: know your computer. With the information in this book as a beginning, delve into *Inside Macintosh*. Really understand how Toolbox calls are executed. Pay particular attention to memory-related issues, because a large percentage of bugs are caused by memory allocation and management problems.

Chapter 9

Becoming a Macintosh Developer

This chapter provides you with some hints on becoming a Macintosh developer. From a technical standpoint, you will want to acquaint yourself with *Inside Macintosh* and learn how to make best use of it in your work. From a business perspective, you will find it helpful to register with Apple as someone who is developing Macintosh applications.

Continuing your Macintosh education

The Macintosh is a powerful system that has been designed to be easy for end users to operate. It does not follow that it is also easy to program. As you have seen in this book, programming the Macintosh requires you to rethink some basic ideas about computers and their operation.

As a result of this relative complexity, you will find yourself in a continuing process of learning more about the Macintosh family and how to program it. For the next steps in that technical education, there are three recommended courses of action. In no particular order they are

☐ reading *Inside Macintosh* judiciously

☐ examining other people's programs

☐ attending one or more Apple training seminars.

Finding your way through *Inside Macintosh*

Because of the marked differences between the Macintosh and other microcomputers, and because of the wide range of powerful Toolbox and Operating System calls, Macintosh documentation for the programmer tends to be extensive. It can seem overwhelming at first to look at the nearly 2,000 pages of *Inside Macintosh*. But, as you have seen in this book, you need not try to memorize or even learn all of the commands and techniques described.

Apple has provided three road maps to make it easier for you to find your way through the manuals:

☐ Appendix B in this book, which lists the most important of the Operating System and Toolbox calls introduced in this book and explains what they do

□ "About Macintosh Technical Documentation" in the preface to this and other books in the collection, which depicts how the various pieces of documentation work together

□ the "road map" chapter of *Inside Macintosh*, Volume I, which explains the structure of individual chapters in the set and provides some guidance on next steps to take

The important calls

The listing in Appendix B was arrived at by talking to dozens of programmers with a collective experience of tens of thousands of lines of Macintosh programming. Many of them are Apple employees responsible for maintaining the pieces of the Operating System and the Toolbox. Others are outside developers who have produced complex and popular applications.

By performing this "triage" of calls for you, this appendix provides you with a good first screening pass for your continued education about Macintosh programming. If a call is listed in Appendix B, it is one with which you should probably have at least a nodding acquaintance. If it is not there, that doesn't mean you'll *never* need it. It means simply that it is not among those that experienced Macintosh programmers find frequently useful.

Guide to the documentation

The preface of this book furnishes a guide to *Inside Macintosh*. It outlines the relationship among the various manuals that make up the suite of Macintosh programming documentation. It also furnishes, in Table P-1, a brief summary of each of the manuals' contents and focus.

Using this information, you can probably focus your search for more information about a particular aspect of Macintosh programming quite quickly. You can also see at a glance where to go for more information about a subject that may be only lightly covered in one of the manuals in the collection.

The road map in *Inside Macintosh*

In the "road map" chapter of *Inside Macintosh,* Volume I, you will find, among other things, an example program (written in a Pascal dialect), a brief explanation of that program, and the section "Where to Go From Here."

By studying the example—a simple program that displays a single window and permits you to edit text in it—and looking at the structure of the code, you can gain a great deal of insight into how Macintosh programming looks and feels.

Then by looking at "Where to Go From Here," you can determine the next sections of *Inside Macintosh* to read for the information you want.

Examining other people's programs

Traditionally, one of the best ways to learn to program in a new language or environment is to find some example programs and "take them apart." In MPW and MacApp (see Chapter 8), as well as many other development environments, sample programs are included. In addition, the MPW environment, MacApp, and many third-party languages and development tools include examples. Sometimes, these programs are well designed and can reveal something about program strategy on the Macintosh. Even when they are not programming gems in their design and structure, they often demonstrate useful techniques.

Quite often, the programmers who develop and make these programs available furnish the source code routinely. Many are willing to provide it on request.

If you are one of those programmers who learns best by taking apart someone else's code, you should have no trouble finding some to dismantle and analyze.

Attending Apple programming seminars

Another good source of technical education for Macintosh developers is the array of seminars and training classes offered by Apple Computer. Ranging from one-day technical overviews to one-week intensive programming experiences, these seminars can help speed you along the road to Macintosh mastery.

More information about these programs can be obtained through Apple Developer Services.

> *" On a more traditional system, the best training for program-ming is the text adventure game, since you spend so much time groping in the dark. The Macintosh Toolbox is the light in that darkness. "*
>
> **Geoff Brown, author of Deluxe Music Construction Set**

Registering as a Macintosh developer

Apple Developer Services can provide you with a great many support functions including

☐ equipment at reduced prices (and sometimes in advance of the equipment's marketing release)

☐ training classes

☐ access to the Apple Evangelists for help in designing, positioning, and marketing the product

☐ on-going technical support during product development

☐ licensing agreements

To obtain information about becoming a certified developer, send a letter to Developer Relations, Mail Stop 27-S, Apple Computer, Inc., 20525 Mariani Ave., Cupertino, CA 95014.

Once you are certified, you will receive regular mailings from Apple, including *TechNotes*, which provide updates about the Macintosh family that may be helpful to you as you develop applications.

❖ *Note:* If you plan to distribute any Apple software—including such things as the System, Finder, or ImageWriter® and LaserWriter® resources—with your programs, then you must become a recognized Apple developer and sign appropriate licensing agreements.

Appendixes

Appendix A

Compatibility Issues and Guidelines

This appendix discusses design and programming considerations involved in ensuring that programs you write will be compatible across all existing Macintosh family product lines. More detailed information on the subject can be found in occasional Macintosh Technical Notes, specifically Notes 2, 7, and 117.

These comments are intended to be guidelines only. If you are designing a program that has a valid reason to deviate from these recommendations, you must only be aware that doing so risks the possibility that your program may not run correctly or at all on future versions of the Macintosh.

Some of the suggestions in this appendix are simply good Macintosh programming guidelines that happen also to have a relationship to compatibility.

For the purpose of this discussion, these tips and guidelines can be divided into five main pieces of advice:

☐ Use system globals, not hard-coded addresses, when possible.

☐ Check errors and don't ignore them when they arise.

☐ Don't rely on things not changing.

☐ Avoid using the system heap zone unnecessarily.

☐ Don't write to or read from Nil handles and pointers.

Use system globals

Wherever they are provided, it is safer to use system globals than to make assumptions about where things are stored and how big they are. This section provides some typical guidance on this topic; the list could be much longer, but you'll get the idea.

Don't assume the screen is a fixed size

You may be tempted to set the boundsRect within which windows can be dragged, or to make other screen-specific assumptions. If you do, the program may not run well, or even at all, on Macintosh systems with other screen sizes. For example, a Macintosh II's screen size depends on the video card and display. It cannot be known in advance. Similarly, the screen on the Macintosh XL is wider than that of the standard Macintosh.

Rather than hard-coding the corners of the bounding rectangle boundsRect, take advantage of the fact that QuickDraw must "know" where the corners are and stores them in a global variable called screenBits.bounds. Assuming QuickDraw has been properly initialized, you can set the boundary rectangle to the size of the screen with a call like this pseudo-code example:

```
boundsRect = screenBits.bounds
```

Regardless of the size screen being used by the system, this kind of call will result in your program staying within the appropriate boundaries.

Don't assume the screen is in a fixed location

The base address of the screen location in memory varies with the model of Macintosh. Rather than hard-coding this address for the machine on which you expect people to run the program, use the QuickDraw global variable screenBits.baseAddr. You can do this with a call like this pseudo-code example:

```
myScreenBase = screenBits.baseAddr
```

Don't assume screen width is in rowBytes

As you learned in Chapter 5, the width of the Macintosh screen can be determined by the value stored in the variable rowBytes. But relying on this as the best way to discover the actual width of the displayable area may lead to problems. If the user owns one of the large-screen displays, for example, he or she may be unable to drag your application's window to some parts of the screen.

Again, two global QuickDraw variables will assist in the process of ensuring that you are assigning these values. The variable screenBits.rowBytes always contains the correct value for the number of bytes wide the current display is, and the variable screenBits.bounds.right always has the right screen size.

Don't make too many assumptions about files

Use the standard `SFGetFile` and `SFPutFile` routines to access disk files rather than directly manipulating file and volume control blocks. This will ensure that your program is compatible with both MFS and HFS file systems without any additional effort on your part.

Check errors returned by calls

Many Macintosh calls return error codes as part of their operation. If your program checks these errors and, in the event of a nonzero code, takes some appropriate action, it will be well on its way to being compatible across model lines.

This suggestion can be restated simply: Always write code that is defensive. As one Macintosh wag says, "Assume that everyone and everything is out to kill you. Trust no one."

Any use of Operating System routines should always check the OSErr they return. Ignoring them or failing to check them can result in painful system crashes that are very difficult to find.

Don't rely on things not changing

In a system as complex and revolutionary as the Macintosh, some evolution over time is inevitable. Couple this truism with Apple's clearly stated intent to continue to expand the Macintosh family and you can see that assuming that anything not clearly fixed in place will remain the same forever is not a good assumption.

Watch copy-protection code closely

The main reason programs fail as they move from one member of the Macintosh family to another is related to copy-protection schemes developers use. Without making any observations about the marketing and ethical issues involved, it is safe to say that if you use a copy-protection scheme that performs sophisticated, tricky, and illegal operations, you greatly increase the risk of incompatibility.

Many copy-protection schemes rely on direct modification of hardware registers or reserved memory locations. Others use techniques involving self-modifying code. Both of these approaches are potentially dangerous in the Macintosh environment.

Don't use reserved bits

Many of the bytes and words identified as parts of Macintosh data structures have unassigned bits in them. There is a temptation, when a programmer needs a flag "just for a few cycles," to steal one of these bits. It is sound advice not to succumb to this temptation. You should consider all unassigned bits as reserved for Apple's future use.

Don't write timing-sensitive code

The clock rate for the Macintosh II is twice that of the other members of the family. Future Macintosh models may run with yet higher clock rates. As a result, it is a good idea to avoid writing code that depends on the clock rate.

If your code requires timing loops, use the `Delay` routine in the Operating System or the `Ticks` routine as a means of controlling timing loops.

Use ASCII to read keyboard input

Although it is possible to read the characters entered at the Macintosh keyboard as key codes rather than standard ASCII codes, it is best not to do so. These codes vary slightly from model to model. In addition, some users may have third-party keyboards that are completely different from those built by Apple Computer.

If you always read keyboard input as ASCII codes, you will not have compatibility problems in future Macintosh products.

Avoid direct printer output

The argument in favor of *reading* ASCII codes from the keyboard should not be extended to *writing* ASCII codes to the printer. Use the Printing Manager for printer output. This will ensure that you are always compatible with AppleTalk-connected printers, locally connected printers, and future versions of printer drivers.

Avoid using the system heap

System heap space tends to be limited. It is not a good idea, therefore, to use the system heap at all. If you must, however, use it only to allocate objects with a size of 32 bytes or less.

This is not only a compatibility issue but a general Macintosh programming suggestion. The system heap should be seen as being "owned" by the system. Your program should only use it sparingly, if at all.

Watch the use of Nil pointers

It is often appropriate or even necessary to pass a Nil pointer or handle to a ROM call. But it is essential that you never read any information from or write any data to the location pointed to by a Nil pointer or handle.

A Nil pointer or handle has a value of 0. Because a pointer is nothing but a location in memory, a Nil pointer is pointing to memory location 0. Motorola reserves for the processor the use of address locations 0 through 3. Any attempt to read or write there can have disastrous consequences.

Appendix B

Important Operating System and Toolbox Calls

This appendix consists of an alphabetical listing of the important Operating System and User Interface Toolbox calls in the Macintosh family. Virtually all of these calls are discussed in this book. Each call is listed, followed in parentheses by the name of the manager or other portion of the system to which it belongs. Below each call's name and manager information is a brief description of the use of the call.

Important   Do not rely solely on the contents of this appendix to understand and use any of these calls. As usual, *Inside Macintosh* is the final authority on the subject of how they work. The explanations provided here are basic and are designed only to enable you to understand the purpose of each call.

If you master the calls in this appendix, you will be well on your way to being able to write professional and usable Macintosh software.

❖*Note:* In this appendix, **boldface** is used in the descriptions to indicate the names of other calls in this appendix, rather than to highlight terms in the glossary.

Alert (Dialog Manager)

Posts an alert box with no icon. All alerts are modeless dialog boxes to which the user must respond. See **CautionAlert, NoteAlert,** and **StopAlert.**

BeginUpdate (Window Manager)

Sets up the visible region (visRgn) of the appropriate window for redrawing, which your program must then handle. Call this when an update event is detected in your main event loop. Must be balanced by a call to **EndUpdate.**

CautionAlert (Dialog Manager)

Posts an alert box with a Caution icon. See **Alert.**

CloseDialog (Dialog Manager)

Removes the appropriate dialog box from the screen and deletes it from the window list, releasing memory in the process.

ClosePicture (QuickDraw)

Tells QuickDraw to stop saving calls and picture comments as the definition of the currently open picture. Must balance each **OpenPicture** call.

CloseRgn (QuickDraw)

Stops the collection of lines and framed shapes, organizes them into a region definition, and saves the resulting region. Must balance each **OpenRgn** call.

CloseWindow (Window Manager)

Removes the indicated window from the screen and deletes it from the window list, releasing memory in the process.

DeleteMenu (Menu Manager)

Deletes a menu with the furnished ID from the current menu list in memory. Call **DrawMenuBar** to redraw the menu with the deleted menu no longer present.

DialogSelect (Dialog Manager)

Handles events in a modeless dialog box, returning a True if the event involves activation of an enabled dialog item, False if it is any other kind of event. Compare **ModalDialog.**

DIBadMount (Disk Initialization Package)

Responds to a disk-inserted event that causes an error, either rejecting the disk or posting a dialog and permitting the user to re-initialize the disk.

DisableItem (Menu Manager)

Disables a specific item in a particular menu. Can also disable the entire menu list for a given menu. Disabled items appear dimmed. See **EnableItem.**

DisposeControl (Control Manager)

Removes the identified control from the screen, deletes it from the window's control list, and releases memory in the process. See **KillControls.**

DisposDialog (Dialog Manager)

Calls **CloseDialog** automatically and then releases the memory occupied by the dialog's item list and dialog record.

DisposeMenu (Menu Manager)

Releases memory occupied by a menu allocated with NewMenu. Don't use this if the menu was added with **GetNewMBar,** in which case you should use **ReleaseResource** instead.

DisposeWindow (Window Manager)

Calls **CloseWindow** automatically and then releases the memory occupied by the window record.

DisposHandle (Memory Manager)

Releases the memory occupied by a relocatable block. Compare **DisposPtr.**

DisposPtr (Memory Manager)

Releases the memory occupied by a nonrelocatable block.
Compare **DisposHandle.**

DragWindow (Window Manager)

Pulls a dotted outline of the selected window around on the
screen, following the movements of the mouse, until the button is
released. When the button is released, calls **MoveWindow** to
redraw the window in its new location.

DrawChar (QuickDraw)

Places the character supplied as a parameter to the right of the
current pen location and advances the pen accordingly. See
DrawString and **DrawText.**

DrawControls (Control Manager)

Draws all of the controls currently visible in the window supplied
as a parameter.

DrawGrowIcon (Window Manager)

In response to an update or activate event involving a window
with a size box, draws the size box. Appearance and location of
the size box depend on how the window is defined. For standard
document windows, it is in the lower right corner of the frame.

DrawMenuBar (Menu Manager)

Redraws the menu bar in accordance with the current menu list,
incorporating any changes since the last time it was called.

DrawPicture (QuickDraw)

Takes the portion of the picture supplied as a parameter that is
located inside the picture frame and draws it in a destination
rectangle also supplied as a parameter. In the process, shrinks or
expands the picture to match the borders of the destination
rectangle.

DrawString (QuickDraw)

Calls **DrawChar** for each character in the string supplied as a parameter. Compare **DrawText.**

DrawText (QuickDraw)

Calls **DrawChar** for each character stored at a location in memory pointed to by a parameter to the call. You may specify the starting and ending bytes to draw from the memory structure.

EnableItem (Menu Manager)

Re-enables a previously disabled item (see **DisableItem**) in a menu. The choice is no longer dimmed.

EndUpdate (Window Manager)

Restores the window supplied as a parameter to its appropriate current state. Must balance each **BeginUpdate** call.

FillRect (QuickDraw)

Fills the rectangle supplied as one parameter with the pattern defined by the other. Applies equally to all other QuickDraw shapes.

FindControl (Control Manager)

Tells the application which, if any, of a window's controls the mouse button was pressed in. Call this when your main event loop reports a mouse-down event in the content region of a window that contains controls.

FindWindow (Window Manager)

Tells the application which, if any, part of the window the mouse button was pressed in. Call this when your main event loop reports a mouse-down event and the location could be a window.

FlushEvents (OS Event Manager)

Removes all or selected events from the event queue depending on whether a mask is supplied and if so what its value is. A mask value of 0 results in all pending events being purged.

FSClose (File Manager)

Removes the file's access path, writes the contents of the volume buffer to the volume, and updates the file entry in the file directory. See **FSOpen.**

FSCreate (File Manager)

Creates a new file with the specified name, file type, and creator, on the specified volume. Sets date and time of creation and last modification.

FSOpen (File Manager)

Creates an access path to the file whose name is furnished as a parameter, on the volume specified as another parameter. The returned file reference number is used in subsequent access to the file.

FSRead (File Manager)

Given a byte count, a file reference number, and a memory buffer location pointer, attempts to read the number of bytes indicated from the named file and place the resulting data in the buffer. Returns the number of bytes actually read to the calling program.

FSWrite (File Manager)

Given a byte count, a file reference number, and a memory buffer location pointer, attempts to write the number of bytes indicated to the named file from the buffer. Returns the number of bytes actually written to the calling program.

GetCtlValue (Control Manager)

Returns the current setting of the indicated control. Used to determine if a control is on or off or what its value is (in the case of scroll bars, for example).

GetCCursor (Color QuickDraw)

The color equivalent of **GetCursor.**

GetCursor (Toolbox Utilities)

Returns a handle to the cursor with the resource ID supplied as a parameter. Calls **GetResource.**

GetEOF (File Manager)

Returns the logical EOF of the open file whose reference number is supplied as a parameter.

GetFontInto (QuickDraw)

Returns basic information about the current graphics port's font.

GetIcon (Toolbox Utilities)

Returns a handle to an icon with the supplied resource ID. Makes an automatic call to **GetResource** to load the icon.

GetItem (Menu Manager)

Returns the text of the given menu item.

GetMenu (Menu Manager)

Returns a menu handle for the menu having the given resource ID. Once you have obtained a menu resource by this method, call **InsertMenu** and **DrawMenuBar** to display it.

GetMenuBar (Menu Manager)

Creates a copy of the current menu list and returns a handle to the copy. Permits modification of the menu, which can then be redisplayed with changes using **SetMenuBar** and **DrawMenuBar.**

GetNewControl (Control Manager)

Creates a control from a control template stored in a resource file, adds it to the beginning of the window's control list, and returns a handle to the newly created control. See **NewControl.**

GetNewDialog (Dialog Manager)

Creates a dialog in accordance with specifications contained in a resource file and having the resource ID supplied as a parameter to the call. See **NewDialog.**

GetNewMBar (Menu Manager)

Creates a new menu list from specifications contained in a resource file. Returns a handle to the new menu list. To make this the current menu list, call **SetMenuBar.**

GetNewWindow (Window Manager)

Creates a window in accordance with specifications contained in a resource file and having the resource ID supplied as a parameter to the call. See **NewWindow.**

GetNextEvent (Event Manager)

The "workhorse" of the Toolbox. Returns the next available event of a specified type or types and removes it from the event queue. Returns information about the event in an event record your program can use to determine how to respond to it.

GetPattern (Toolbox Utilities)

Returns a handle to the pattern with the resource ID supplied as a parameter.

GetPen (QuickDraw)

Returns the location of the pen.

GetPenState (QuickDraw)

Returns the location, size, pattern, and mode of the pen. Used primarily to permit your program to save the current state of the pen before it changes it temporarily. See **SetPenState.**

GetPicture (Toolbox Utilities)

Returns a handle to the picture with the resource ID supplied as a parameter.

GetPort (QuickDraw)

Returns a pointer to the current graphics port. See **SetPort.**

GetResource (Resource Manager)

Returns a handle to the resource having the type and ID supplied as parameters. Reads it from a file if necessary, but if the resource is already in memory, simply returns a handle to it with no disk access taking place. Used by many of the other Toolbox calls to find a resource.

GlobalToLocal (QuickDraw)

Converts the point supplied as a parameter from global coordinates (upper left bit image as coordinate (0,0)) into local coordinates of the current graphics port. Compare **LocalToGlobal.**

GrowWindow (Window Manager)

Pulls a grow image of the window around, following the mouse movements, until the button is released. Returns the size of the current graphics port. When the user releases the mouse button, call **SizeWindow** to change the window to its new size.

HideControl (Control Manager)

Makes the control whose handle is passed as a parameter invisible. See **ShowControl.**

HideCursor (QuickDraw)

Removes the cursor from the screen and decrements the cursor level by 1. Only when the cursor level is 0 will the cursor be visible. Must be balanced with a call to **ShowCursor.** See **ObscureCursor.**

InitCursor (QuickDraw)

Sets the current cursor to the standard arrow shape and sets the cursor level to 0, making the cursor visible.

InitDialogs (Dialog Manager)

Initializes the Dialog Manager. Call once before any Dialog Manager calls are executed.

InitFonts (Font Manager)

Initializes the Font Manager. Call once before any Font Manager calls are executed.

InitGraf (QuickDraw)

Initializes QuickDraw. Call once before any QuickDraw calls are executed.

InitMenus (Menu Manager)

Initializes the Menu Manager. Call once before any Menu Manager calls are executed.

InitWindows (Window Manager)

Initializes the Window Manager. Call once before any Window Manager calls are executed.

InsertMenu (Menu Manager)

Searches through all open resource files for menu resources and inserts these resource names in the menu where specified in a parameter.

InvertRect (QuickDraw)

Inverts the pixels in the specified rectangle, converting each white pixel to black and each black pixel to white. Applies equally to the other QuickDraw shapes.

IsDialogEvent (Dialog Manager)

Determines whether an event that takes place while a modeless dialog box is available to the user should be handled as part of that dialog box's processing. Returns a Boolean True if the event is related to the dialog box, False if it is not.

KillControls (Control Manager)

Disposes of all controls associated with the window passed as a parameter. See **DisposeControl.**

Line (QuickDraw)

Draws a line to a point relative to the current position of the pen, using increments for horizontal and vertical position supplied as parameters. Compare **LineTo.**

LineTo (QuickDraw)

Draws a line from the current pen position to the point whose coordinates are supplied as parameters. Compare **Line.**

LocalToGlobal (QuickDraw)

Converts the point supplied as a parameter from the current graphics port's local coordinates into the screen's global coordinate system. In global coordinates, the upper left corner of the graphics port becomes location (0,0). Compare **GlobalToLocal.**

MenuChoice (Menu Manager)

Available only in System version 4.1 and higher. If a menu processing command (**MenuKey** or **MenuSelect**) returns a 0, call this to find out what dimmed menu choice the user may have tried to access.

MenuKey (Menu Manager)

Translates a Command-key combination into the corresponding menu choice if one exists.

MenuSelect (Menu Manager)

Handles the mouse while it is located in the menu bar. Keeps track of where the mouse is, highlighting menus and items as appropriate. Returns a value your program can decode to determine where the user released the mouse and therefore what menu choice should be processed.

ModalDialog (Dialog Manager)

Repeatedly gets and handles events in the window of a modal dialog box. Returns the dialog box item chosen by the user for your program to process.

Move (QuickDraw)

Relocates the pen relative to its current position and according to the horizontal and vertical increments supplied as parameters. No drawing takes place as the pen moves. Compare **Line** and **MoveTo.**

MoveControl (Control Manager)

Relocates the control specified as a parameter to a new location in its window, with its upper left corner located at the coordinates supplied as parameters.

MoveTo (QuickDraw)

Relocates the pen from its current position to the point whose coordinates are supplied as parameters. No drawing takes place as the pen moves. Compare **LineTo** and **Move.**

MoveWindow (Window Manager)

Moves the currently active window (or another window whose pointer is supplied as an argument) to another part of the screen, relocating its upper left corner and positioning the rest of the window in accordance with its size, which is unchanged by the move.

NewControl (Control Manager)

Creates a control and adds it to the specified window's control list, returning a handle to the new control. Compare **GetNewControl.**

NewDialog (Dialog Manager)

Creates a new dialog box as specified by its parameters and returns a pointer to the new dialog. Compare **GetNewDialog.**

NewHandle (Memory Manager)

Allocates a block of memory of the specified size and returns a handle to its location. Call this to create relocatable blocks. Compare **NewPtr.**

NewPtr (Memory Manager)

Allocates a block of memory of the specified size and returns a pointer to its location. Call this to create nonrelocatable blocks. Compare **NewHandle.**

NewRgn (QuickDraw)

Allocates space for a new, variable-sized region, initializes it to the empty region defined by the rectangle (0,0)(0,0), and returns a handle to the new region. Must be used before any region operations (such as **OpenRgn**) can be performed.

NewWindow (Window Manager)

Creates a window as specified by its parameters, adds it to the window list, and returns a pointer to it. Compare **GetNewWindow.**

NoteAlert (Dialog Manager)

Invokes an alert and posts a modal dialog box with the predefined Note icon and an appropriate message. See **Alert.**

ObscureCursor (QuickDraw)

Hides the cursor until the next time the mouse is moved. Normally called when the user begins to type. Compare **HideCursor.**

OpenPicture (QuickDraw)

Returns a handle to a new picture framed by the rectangle supplied as a parameter. Initiates the saving of all drawing routines and picture comments, if any, as the picture definition. See **DrawPicture.**

OpenRgn (QuickDraw)

Tells QuickDraw to allocate temporary space and begin saving lines and framed shapes for later processing as a region definition. Must be preceded by a call to **NewRgn.**

PaintRect (QuickDraw)

Paints the specified rectangle with the current graphics port's pen pattern and mode. Compare **FillRect.** Equally applicable to all QuickDraw shapes.

PenMode (QuickDraw)

Sets the transfer mode through which a pen pattern will be transferred onto an existing bit map when lines or shapes are drawn. Determines the appearance of drawing over existing graphic objects, shapes, and lines. Initially set to patCopy and can be reset to this value by a call to **PenNormal.**

PenNormal (QuickDraw)

Resets the initial state of the pen in the current graphics port so that it is one pixel by one pixel (see **PenSize**), in the patCopy transfer mode (see **PenMode**), and in black (see **PenPat**).

PenPat (QuickDraw)

Sets the pattern with which the pen will draw in the current graphics port. Initially set to black and can be reset to black by a call to **PenNormal.**

PenSize (QuickDraw)

Sets the size of the pen in the current graphics port to a width and height in pixels as specified by parameters to the call. Initially set to (1,1) and can be reset to that value by a call to **PenNormal.**

PlotIcon (Toolbox Utilities)

Draws the icon whose handle is furnished as a parameter in the rectangle furnished as the other parameter.

ReleaseResource (Resource Manager)

Releases the memory, if any, allocated to the resource whose handle is supplied as a parameter. Use only after you are completely through with a resource.

SelectWindow (Window Manager)

Makes the window whose pointer is passed as a parameter the active window by unhighlighting the presently active window, bringing the desired window to the top of the stack, highlighting it, and generating appropriate activate events. Usually called when a mouse-down event is detected in the content region of an inactive window.

SetCCursor (Color QuickDraw)

The color equivalent of **SetCursor.**

SetCursor (QuickDraw)

Sets the current cursor to the cursor supplied as an argument. Does not change the visibility of the cursor.

SetEOF (File Manager)

Sets the logical EOF of the open file whose reference number is supplied as a parameter, to the position specified as the other parameter. An attempt to set the logical EOF beyond the physical EOF sets the logical EOF one byte past the next free allocation block. Using a logical EOF of 0 releases all disk spaced occupied by the file.

SetFPos (File Manager)

Sets the mark of the open file whose reference number is supplied as a parameter, to the position specified.

SetItem (Menu Manager)

Changes the text of the given menu item to the text supplied as a parameter. Useful in toggling menus.

SetMenuBar (Menu Manager)

Makes the menu list whose handle is supplied as a parameter the current menu list. Particularly useful when a previous call to **GetMenuBar** has stored a menu your program has temporarily replaced or removed. Call **DrawMenuBar** to display the new menu.

SetOrigin (QuickDraw)

Changes the local coordinate system of the current graphics port. Upper left corner coordinates of the graphics port's rectangle are set to the parameters supplied. All subsequent drawing takes place with reference to this new origin value. Particularly useful after a scrolling operation.

SetPenState (QuickDraw)

Sets the pen location, size, pattern, and mode in the current graphics port to the values supplied as parameters. Compare **GetPenState.**

SetPort (QuickDraw)

Makes the port supplied as a parameter the current graphics port.

SFGetFile (Standard File Package)

Displays a dialog box listing the names of a specific group of files from which the user can select one to be opened. Repeatedly gets and handles events until the user confirms the command after choosing a filename or aborts by clicking Cancel. Returns the user's action in a reply record.

SFPutFile (Standard File Package)

Displays a dialog box allowing the user to specify a file to which data will be written during a Save or Save As command's execution. Repeatedly gets and handles events until the user either confirms the command after entering an appropriate filename or aborts the command by clicking Cancel. Returns the user's action in a reply record.

ShowControl (Control Manager)

Makes the specified control visible. If it's already visible, has no effect. Used in conjunction with **HideControl.**

ShowCursor (QuickDraw)

Increments the cursor level by 1. If the cursor level is already 0, has no effect and the cursor remains visible. If, however, one or more previous calls to **HideCursor** have decremented the cursor level below 0, each call to ShowCursor increases the level by 1 until it reaches 0. Balancing of these two calls is required.

SizeControl (Control Manager)

Changes the size of the specified control's enclosing rectangle. The upper left corner of the rectangle remains anchored, and the lower right corner is adjusted as appropriate. Useful when a window containing controls is resized by the user.

SizeWindow (Window Manager)

Enlarges or shrinks the specified window's graphics port's rectangle to the width and height specified as parameters.

SpaceExtra (QuickDraw)

Specifies the average number of pixels by which to widen each space in a line of text in the current graphics port. Useful when displaying fully justified text.

StopAlert (Dialog Manager)

Invokes an alert and posts a modal dialog box with the predefined Stop icon and an appropriate message. See **Alert.**

SystemClick (Desk Manager)

Determines which part of a desk accessory's window the mouse button was pressed in and responds accordingly. Call this when your main event loop detects a mouse-down event and the **FindWindow** routine reports that the event took place in a system window.

TEClick (TextEdit)

Controls the placement and highlighting of the selection range in a TextEdit field. Call this whenever a mouse-down event occurs in the view rectangle of the edit record. Keeps control until the user releases the mouse button.

TECopy (TextEdit)

Copies the text in the selection range into TextEdit's local scrap. If the selection range is an insertion point, the scrap is emptied. Otherwise, the selected text completely replaces the contents of the local scrap.

TECut (TextEdit)

Removes the text in the selection range from the specified text and places it into TextEdit's local scrap. Text is redrawn as necessary. If the selection range is an insertion point, the scrap is emptied. Otherwise, the selected text completely replaces the contents of the local scrap.

TEDelete (TextEdit)

Same as **TECut** except that the removed text is not placed in the local scrap, whose contents are unaffected.

TEDispose (TextEdit)

Releases the memory allocated for the edit record and text specified by the parameter. Call this only when you are completely finished using an edit record.

TEInit (TextEdit)

Initializes TextEdit and allocates a handle for its scrap. Call this once before any TextEdit routines are executed.

TEInsert (TextEdit)

Inserts the text whose handle is provided as a parameter just before the selection range or insertion point in the indicated text field, redrawing text as needed. Current selection range and scrap are unaffected.

TEKey (TextEdit)

Places the character passed as a parameter in the text field supplied as the other parameter, replacing the selection range or inserting at the insertion point. Redraws the text as necessary.

TENew (TextEdit)

Allocates a handle for text, creates and initializes an edit record, and returns a handle to the new edit record. Use this once for each new edit record you want to allocate.

TEPaste (TextEdit)

Replaces the current selection range in the specified text field with the contents of the TextEdit local scrap, leaving the insertion point just past the newly inserted text. Text is redrawn as necessary. Contents of the scrap remain unchanged.

TextBox (TextEdit)

Creates an uneditable text field containing text whose pointer is supplied as a parameter. Frequently used in designing dialogs.

TextFace (QuickDraw)

Sets the current graphics port's character style to one or more of the predefined constants bold, italic, underline, outline, shadow, condense, and extend.

TextFont (QuickDraw)

Sets the current graphics port's font to the font number supplied as a parameter. Font number 0 is the system font and is the default.

TextMode (QuickDraw)

Sets the current graphics port's transfer mode for drawing text. The mode determines the appearance of text drawn over existing graphics objects and shapes. See **PenMode.**

TextSize (QuickDraw)

Sets the size of the current graphics port's font to the number of points in the parameter. A parameter of 0 instructs QuickDraw to use the system font size, 12 point.

TrackControl (Control Manager)

Follows the movements of the mouse and responds appropriately until the button is released. Call this when the user presses the mouse button in a visible, active control, to ensure that the user does not change his or her mind about activating the control. Also tracks the movement of scroll bars and their associated moving parts.

TrackGoAway (Window Manager)

Keeps control until the user releases the mouse button, highlighting the close box as long as the mouse is positioned inside it, and unhighlighting it when the mouse moves outside it. Use this to ensure that the user does not change his or her mind about closing a window.

UnloadSeg (Segment Loader)

Marks a code segment as being relocatable and purgeable. Block is not actually purged or moved unless the Memory Manager must do so to allocate new memory.

Appendix C

The Apple Programmer's and Developer's Association (APDA)

In the summer of 1986, Apple Computer and the A.P.P.L.E. Co-Op of Renton, Washington, jointly formed the Apple Programmer's and Developer's Association (APDA). The purpose of this organization is to provide a vehicle through which individuals programming applications for the Macintosh family and for the rest of Apple's product line can obtain technical information and development tools.

During the first year of its existence, APDA saw its membership swell to 15,000.

If you are going to develop applications for the Macintosh family, you will almost certainly want to join APDA.

What APDA provides

Membership in APDA entitles you to receive a quarterly newsletter, *APDAlog*, which provides information on the latest releases of Apple and third-party software development tools, utilities, books, and other programmer-related products.

In addition, you will receive *TechNotes* from Apple Computer, early releases of software and documentation (often before Apple Computer releases the same materials to the general public), and access to an automatic ordering process that guarantees you will always have the latest version of the software with which you work every day.

APDA members can contact the association through many on-line services, including CompuServe, AppleLink®, GEnie, and MCI Mail, for orders and technical product information.

How to join APDA

Membership in APDA is open to anyone who completes and signs a membership application and pays the $20 annual membership fee. Write to

Apple Programmer's and Developer's Association
290-SW 43rd Street
Renton, WA 98055
(206) 251-6548

The application includes provisions indicating that the member understands the strictures against distributing certain Apple software that may be obtained through APDA.

Apple encourages you to become involved in APDA as a means of gaining technical information and early access to programming products you will need to make you a successful Macintosh developer.

Glossary

alert: A warning or report of an error in the form of an alert box, a sound from the computer's speaker, or both. See **alert box.**

alert box: A box that appears on the screen to give a warning or to report an error message during the use of an application. There are three types of alert boxes on the Macintosh. In increasing order of severity, they are Note, Caution, and Stop.

ancestor: In object-oriented programming, a class or object from which the class or object under consideration is derived or from which it inherits traits. See **descendant.**

application file: A file containing an application program. Compare **document file.**

application heap: The part of the **heap** set aside for an application's use.

application space: Same as **application heap.**

bit image: A collection of bits in memory that have a rectilinear representation. The display on the screen is a visible bit image.

bit map: A set of bits that represent the position and state of a corresponding set of items. See **pixel.**

bit-mapped graphics: A method of graphic representation in which each **pixel** on a display corresponds to a bit in memory, allowing each pixel to be individually controlled.

block: An arbitrary section of memory, generally understood to be made up of contiguous locations.

boundary rectangle: The coordinates of the upper left and lower right corners of a rectangle making up the outside edges, typically of a **bit map** or a **graphics port.**

built-in command: A command included in the User Interface Toolbox or elsewhere in system-level software furnished by Apple with the Macintosh.

bundling: The process whereby a specific type of document file is operationally connected to an application so that when the user opens the document, the appropriate application is automatically selected and run.

CGrafPort: The data type for a color graphics port. Also shorthand for **color graphics port.**

close box: Same as **go-away region.**

color graphics port: A complete drawing environment that contains all the necessary information for Color QuickDraw to carry out instructions. See **graphics port.**

command file: In the Macintosh Programmer's Workshop environment, a file containing a script of commands to be executed as a group when the file is activated.

command interpreter: The part of the Macintosh Programmer's Workshop that executes commands passed to it by the programmer or other parts of the MPW system.

content region: The part of a window into which the user or the application is expected to place text or graphics information.

control: Part of a window or dialog box that is active and through which the user can control certain aspects of a program's operation. These include scroll bars, size boxes, zoom boxes, close boxes, buttons, and check boxes.

Control Manager: The part of the Toolbox responsible for managing the manipulation of **controls** in windows and dialog boxes.

creator: A four-character identifier that facilitates the identification of the application that generated a document file. Used to identify a file's application as part of the process of **bundling.**

cursor level: At any time, the cursor being used in an application has a level associated with it. This level determines whether the cursor is visible or invisible. Hiding the cursor decrements its level by 1; instructing that it be shown increases the level by 1. Only a cursor with a level of 0 is visible.

customize: In object-oriented programming, declaring or defining an immediate descendant of a class or object. The process creates a new instance of the class or object, which may in turn be given special characteristics.

data fork: The part of a Macintosh file that contains nonresource information. Compare **resource fork.**

dereferencing: In Pascal, the process by which a **pointer** is converted into an absolute memory address. A single caret (^) is used to dereference a pointer. Compare **double dereferencing.**

descendant: In object-oriented programming, an object or class derived from the object or class under consideration. See **ancestor.**

destination rectangle: The boundary rectangle within which text in a TextEdit record will be fit, using wrapping if necessary.

dialog: Same as **dialog box.**

dialog box: A box that contains a message requesting more information from the user. A dialog box can be modal (requiring the user to furnish a response before proceeding) or modeless (permitting the user to access other windows without disposing of it first).

Dialog Manager: The part of the Toolbox responsible for displaying and managing **dialog boxes.**

document file: A file containing information to be used by an **application file.**

double dereferencing: In Pascal, the process by which a **handle** is converted into an absolute memory address. Two carets (^^) are used to double dereference a handle.

drag region: The part of a window that causes the window to be moved with the mouse pointer as long as the mouse button is held down. Most of the top portion of a window is the drag region.

editor: A program that helps you create and edit information of a particular form; for example, a text editor or a graphics editor.

edit record: A TextEdit data structure in which information about a text field subject to being edited is stored.

Event Manager: The part of the Toolbox that sorts, filters, and passes interaction with events to running applications and to other parts of the Toolbox.

event queue: The place in memory where the Event Manager stores events as they accumulate so that the program can handle them when the time is appropriate.

field: In programming, one discrete variable within a **record.**

file type: A four-character code assigned to any file by the program that creates it. A file type generally has meaning only within the context of the application.

Finder: An application that's generally always available on the desktop. The user manages documents and applications, and gets information to and from disks via the Finder.

fork: A generic name for one of two portions of a Macintosh file. All such files contain two bit streams, or forks. One is the **resource fork** and the other is the **data fork.** Either may be empty in any given file.

fragmentation: The process whereby the **application heap** becomes a series of disjointed allocation blocks. This condition can make it difficult or even impossible to allocate new memory when it is needed, even though the total amount of available space may be adequate to do so.

global coordinate system: The coordinate system associated with a bit image and independent of any bit map or graphics port's defining boundary rectangle. Used to transfer information about the locations of objects between applications or between parts of an application with different **local coordinate systems.**

go-away region: The small box usually located in the upper left corner of a window. By clicking this region, the user can cause the window to disappear from the desktop.

grafPort: The data type for a graphics port. Also shorthand for **graphics port.**

graphics port: The complete environment within which QuickDraw graphics routines are carried out on the classic Macintosh.

grow region: The small control usually in the lower right corner of a window. By dragging on this region, the user can resize a window. Not all windows have grow regions.

handle: An address that points to another address, where a **pointer** to a particular block of memory is located. Handles enable the program to locate relocatable objects.

heap: The region of memory in which space is allocated and deallocated explicitly, either by the running program (in the case of the **application heap**) or by the system (in the case of the **system heap**). Compare **stack.**

heap zone: An independently managed and allocated portion of a **heap.** It is possible to divide the application heap into multiple application heap zones.

hot spot: The particular pixel on a cursor that is used to determine the location of the cursor on the screen. All cursors must have only one such zone.

library: A collection of routines, procedures, functions, or other programming modules. The User Interface Toolbox is a library.

local coordinate system: A coordinate system in which the location of the origin (0,0) is determined by the **boundary rectangle** of the specific bit map. Compare **global coordinate system.**

Macintosh Programmer's Workshop (MPW): A Macintosh development environment marketed by Apple through the Apple Programmer's and Developer's Association.

makefile: A file in a development environment like the Macintosh Programmer's Workshop that contains compiler or assembler commands to create an executable, linked file of object code from source code files, libraries, and other needed resources.

mark: The current position marker maintained by the File Manager to keep track of where it is in the file during a read or write operation.

mask: A pattern used to screen out certain types of events in the **Event Manager.** The pattern consists of the sum of the numeric values associated with the mask for each type of event an application need not acknowledge or deal with during its execution.

Memory Manager: The part of the Toolbox that handles the allocation, deallocation, relocation, and manipulation of blocks of memory space.

menu definition procedure: A procedure for creating nonstandard types of menus, generally written in assembly language. Used only by applications that require a menu of a type other than that supplied in the Toolbox routines. Also called a *menu defproc.*

menu list: A list of handles to one or more menus, along with information about the position of each menu in the menu bar.

Menu Manager: The part of the Toolbox responsible for the display, update, and response to user events in the menu bar and the pull-down menus of the Macintosh.

method: In **object-oriented** programming, roughly equivalent to a procedure in **procedure-oriented** programming. A set of instructions to be carried out when a particular **object** receives a message with the same name as the method.

MPW: Abbreviation for **Macintosh Programmer's Workshop.**

MPW Shell: The general Macintosh Programmer's Workshop development environment, including the editor and tools but exclusive of the languages used to develop an application.

nonrelocatable object: A block of memory that has been declared in such a way that its position is stored in a **pointer.** The Memory Manager will not relocate any such object. Excessive use of nonrelocatable objects is discouraged in the Macintosh because of the problem of fragmentation that frequently results.

object: In **object-oriented** programming, any combination of data and the **methods** that operate on that data.

object-oriented: A programming method in which data and procedures (called **methods** in object-oriented programming) are combined rather than separated as in the more traditional **procedure-oriented** programming model.

operating system: A program that organizes the actions of the parts of the computer and its peripheral devices. The Macintosh Operating System is located primarily in ROM and handles low-level tasks such as memory management, serial port control, and disk input and output.

part code: In the **Control Manager,** a code that identifies each specific part of a multipart control.

pattern: An eight-by-eight-bit array of pixels that defines a repeating design or tone. A pattern is used in QuickDraw graphics with the graphics pen and with instructions that fill a shape with a pattern.

picture: In QuickDraw graphics, a collection of calls to routines that draw a **bit image.** Pictures provide a means for one program to draw a shape or collection of shapes defined in another program without knowledge of what the shape is or how it was originally created.

pixel: Short for *picture element.* A point on the graphics screen; the visual representation of a bit on the screen (white if the bit is 0, black if it's 1). Also a location in video memory that maps to a point on the graphics screen when the viewing window includes that location.

pixel image: The color equivalent of a **bit image.**

pixel map: The color equivalent of a **bit map.**

pixel pattern: The color equivalent of a **pattern.**

point: A single location on the Macintosh screen, typically located in a graphics port, and defined by its two address coordinates. Lines and shapes are defined by the points at which they begin and end.

pointer: An address that points directly to a block of memory. Pointers are associated with **nonrelocatable objects.** Compare **handle.**

polygon: In QuickDraw graphics, any sequence of connected lines treated as a continuous shape.

procedure-oriented: An approach to programming in which the data and the procedures that operate on the data are viewed and treated separately. Compare **object-oriented.**

purge: To remove from memory. Only blocks of memory that have been marked as purgeable by the program may be purged by the Memory Manager.

region: In QuickDraw graphics, any collection of bits in a **bit image,** no matter how discontinuous, treated as a single graphic entity on which various graphic and mathematical operations may be performed.

reply record: A data record containing the results of an operation or procedure.

ResEdit: A program supplied by Apple Computer for the management and manipulation of **resources.** With this program, resources can be defined, edited, and moved between applications.

resource: A unit or collection of information used by an application program. Resources are generally stored in the resource fork of a file and loaded into memory when needed by the application. Most objects in the Macintosh environment are resources.

resource fork: The part of a Macintosh file where **resources** are stored. Compare **data fork.**

resource ID: A unique identification number within a type. Each **resource** in an application has associated with it a resource type and a resource ID.

resource map: The first part of the resource fork of a Macintosh file. The map contains information that permits the application to retrieve any individual **resource** as needed without having to search through all of the resources to find the desired one.

resource name: Each **resource,** when it is created, is given a name by the application. The program may then refer to the resource by this name or by its resource ID and resource type.

resource type: A four-character code defining the classification of a **resource.** Apple Computer maintains a registry of these codes to ensure no conflicts arise between applications.

Segment Loader: The part of the Operating System that permits you to divide your application into several parts and have only one or some of them in memory at a time.

stack: The place in memory where temporary values associated with a program's procedures and functions are stored. Compare **heap.**

structure region: An entire window, including its content region and its frame, with any associated controls.

style record: On the Macintosh II, a data structure optionally associated with an **edit record.** It contains data from which TextEdit can obtain information about the font, style, size, and color of text in a TextEdit window.

system heap: The part of the heap set aside for use by the system. Compare **application heap.**

TextEdit: A part of the Toolbox useful for displaying, editing, and managing small amounts of text, usually in **dialog boxes.**

Toolbox: The shorthand way of referring to the **User Interface Toolbox.**

User Interface Toolbox: A collection of built-in commands for managing the interaction between an application and the system. Also called the Toolbox, this part of the Macintosh ROM, sometimes supplemented by disk-based routines, is divided into several managers and packages. See, for example, **Dialog Manager** or **Control Manager.**

view rectangle: The boundary rectangle for a TextEdit record in which the currently editable record can be seen. It provides for no wrapping of text. Compare **destination rectangle.**

volume: A collection of files logically grouped together. A volume is usually an individual disk, although a single disk may contain multiple volumes.

volume reference number: A number automatically assigned by the File Manager when a volume is mounted and guaranteed to be unique throughout the running of an application program. Most file operations are performed by calling the volume by this number rather than by its name and directory path.

Window Manager: The part of the Toolbox dedicated to managing the display of windows on the Macintosh desktop.

zone: A separately managed portion of a heap. See **heap zone.**

Index

THE APPLE PUBLISHING SYSTEM

This Apple manual was written, edited, and composed on a desktop publishing system using the Apple Macintosh® Plus and Microsoft® Word. Proof and final pages were created on the Apple LaserWriter® Plus. POSTSCRIPT®, the LaserWriter's page-description language, was developed by Adobe Systems Incorporated.

Text type is ITC Garamond® (a downloadable font distributed by Adobe Systems). Display type is ITC Avant Garde Gothic®. Bullets are ITC Zapf Dingbats®. Program listings are set in Apple Courier, a monospaced font.

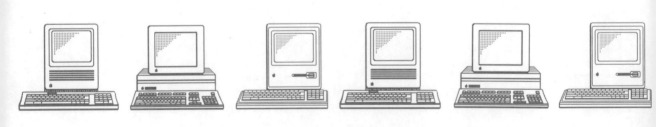